ENHEDUANNA

D1739373

ALİ ERYILMAZ

FA PUBLICATIONS NOVEL SERIES 02

Publisher Certificate Number: 51664

First Edition - November 2021

ENHEDUANNA – ALİ ERYILMAZ

FA KİTAP YAYINCILIK YAPIMCILIK İTH. İHR. LTD. ŞTİ.

Diriliş Mah Güldere Cad S8 B Blok (1/21) Kat: 4

Daire: 18 Mamak/ANKARA

Tel: +90 533 046 24 53

E-mail: fayayinlari@gmail.com

Layout Design: BES CREATİVE

Cover Design: BES CREATİVE

Social Media Advisor: BES CREATİVE

Translator: Mustafa AGCAN

Printing and Cover: Ayrıntı Basım Yayım A.Ş.

Serifika No: 49599

ISBN: 9798758479643

ENHEDUANNA

ALİ ERYILMAZ

A deep silence absorbed the whole temple and its surroundings after a tiring day. Enheduanna had laid down on her sofa knitted from reeds, leaned her head back, stretched out her legs, fixed her eyes on the ceiling and lost in deep thoughts to relax. She was so tired that she had not even thought of taking off her ruby-trimmed crown adorned with thin scaly gold leaves and her scarf that covered her head.

It had just been four years since her father, King Sargon, sent her as a high priestess to this temple located in the city of Ur. During this period, Enheduanna had learned the working of the temple and even realized some wrongs and abuses in its working system. She had tried to deal with each problem one by one and corrected them all, also known the people working in the temple. When she first came, she had realized that the walls surrounding the city of Ur are insufficient for defence and built additional walls surrounding the whole city and towers where soldiers were placed in every fifty meters. She had the workers built two inns so that the merchants could stay who came to Ur for the purpose of trade, supported social life by building houses of adobe bricks for the families living in the houses that made of reeds in bad conditions. She had accepted homeless children to the temple and ensured that they were looked after as the children of Inanna. She had fed the widows and their children in the temple every day, renovated the military guard completely and had the phrase 'Fight Like A God' written on its forefront wall. Enheduanna had sworn to make the city of Ur and the temple as the flower of the kingdom.

The temple was a huge four-storey construction which was sixty meters in length and forty meters in width located in the very center of the city. Each floor rose by covering a smaller area than the previous one and there were very beautiful gardens consisting of cypress trees and flowers. There were three gardens, two small and one large, that included the temple. These areas were used for various purposes and were surrounded by long and strong walls including the temple. On the outer border of the walls, there were one-or two-storey adobe houses where the priests and the priestesses in charge of the temple first, and then other Sumerians lived. The houses were adjacent to each other. This temple was built by King Sargon especially for his daughter Enheduanna and Princess Enheduanna was appointed as the high priestess of the temple. At the entrance of the temple, the following lines were embroidered in the inscription that written and placed by Enheduanna:

I am Enheduanna
A gift basket in hand and
With beautiful songs in my tongue
I made sure the temple was fine
Stacking each brick with offering ceremonies
I made it to the highest
I recreated The Temple of Ur

From the walls of the temple to its corridors in the interior, everywhere was covered with ceramic-coated bricks, in which the powders obtained from lapis lazuli stone were also used. The inner and outer walls were decorated with huge reliefs. The depictions of kings and gods, religious ceremonies, wars and hunting scenes were usually pictured on reliefs. Some of the walls were used as Sumerian annuals, and important political events of the period were depicted on them.

7

Enheduanna could easily read all kinds of tablets thanks to the high education she had taken under the auspices of his father and memorize what she read with her sharp intelligence and memory. She was one of the most well-educated and cultured people of her time. She could engage in ambitious arguments even with the best-trained teachers and scholars in temples and she often was the winner of them. If she was able to wield a weapon a little, she could have taken away the right to become the first heir to the throne from his older brother Rimus.

With her long heights, thin and delicate body, her fringe, braided hair, filled and lively breasts, and slightly wide hips, she had become the favourite of everyone in he city since she arrived. Until Enheduanna came to city of Ur, people of Ur hadn't seen such a beautiful princess and high priestess. Enheduanna had learned the necessity of being beautiful and being beautiful itself from her beloved Goddess Inanna.

She had to act like her goddess to become the favourite of the goddess. She had to pay attention of everything, such as from eating to walking, and caring to working. After all, she was the high priestess of the Goddess in that temple. She had to represent Inanna in the best way, both her success in her work and her beauty in the public eye.

When Enheduanna lay down, half asleep, half awake, she realized that the couch she was lying on was rising slowly and moving towards the sky. She tried to figure out what was going on by moving her eyes around and up and down. The city of Ur was getting smaller and smaller below her. She started to watch the lights of the stars floating through the darkness of the void. The moon was about to become full moon in the sky and counting down its final days for it. But the couch was going on its movement towards Enlil's sky without stopping. A light breeze was blowing the hem of her one-piece dress she was wearing, some of which was thrown over her shoulder.

The couch on which Enheduanna was standing, crossing the lands she had previously travelled and heard from her brother, stood on a high rock at the top of a mountain at last. She felt cold and began to tremble slightly. It was definitely colder here than the city of Ur. And she was definitely at a higher point. Just as she asked to herself, "What is this place?" and "What am I doing here?", she saw a beam of light descending from the sky, right through the moon. She got flustered, and her heart started beating fast. As the beam of light approached her, beats of her heart became faster. She felt like her heart was going to dislocate. She closed her eyes for a while and took a deep breath. She held her breath for a few seconds and then let it out again. She was afraid to open her eyes. She couldn't even imagine what she was going to see in front of her.

"She thought, "Am I cursed?". But what could she have done to anger the Gods? After all, it had just been four years since she became the high priestess. She wondered whether the altars were being cleaned or not. Or were the gifts that presented not enough? Or weren't the instrumentalists and the dancers able to entertain the Gods sufficiently? Was she put on trial before the Gods because of a reason that she didn't know? If so, it was certain that her situation wouldn't be good at all.

As dozens of intriguing questions raced through her mind successively, she felt a hand, warm and soft as velvet, taking her right hand. She slightly raised her eyelids with curiosity and concern. There stood the most beautiful woman she had ever seen so far and she stared at her. The woman was none other than Inanna, to whom she prayed and dreamed of constantly. But how could it be? Inanna, The Great Light that descended from the sky, the Lioness of Heaven, the goddess of all divine powers, was holding her hand now. She was so immersed in Inanna's beauty that, she came to herself by the voice she heard:

"I am the light in you, the love in your heart, the fire in your body, the wine in your veins, the one who makes the seed grown ears and the pen written. I am Inanna!" Are you ready, the chosen man of Inanna who is the sole owner of the Heavens and the earth?''

Enheduanna didn't know what to say, her mouth was dry because of excitement and she became speechless. It was as if she had lost the ability to think. And involuntarily she could say;

''I am ready, the owner of all powers; the moon-faced light of my night that pierces the darkness!''

Enheduanna was inhaling Inanna's voice. It was like the smell of rare flowers; pleasant, soft, and unique... The Goddess said:

''Do not be afraid, this is the Mount Mada, the mountain of the Gods. I brought you here because I chose you among the people for myself. You are my shadow on Earth, the light of my wisdom, the mirror of my beauty. You are the messenger of the sole owner of the Earth, the pen of my greatness. Now, you will remove all the gods in your temple, and make it special only to me. You will write all the prayers and poems that I have inspired you, and make them read in your country. I will give blessings to your people and victory in wars. They will pray to me and only ask of me. They'll present all the gifts to me and give birth their children for me. They'll throw me the seed they have sown in the field, spread the lambs in my pasture. They'll make their beer from my barley and drink it for me. They'll marry to women and make love for me. They'll sweat for me while plowing their fields. They'll say all the good words for me. They'll have fun, and also eat and drink for me.''

While Enheduanna was looking at Inanna's uni - form nose proportional to her face, her full fiery red lips, her spike-blonde wavy hair hanging from under her scarf, her unique-colored eyes like a window opening to the universe, Inanna held both hands of Enheduanna and touched them to her chest. Enheduanna was about to pass out, feeling the goddess's warmth, magnificent form of the epitome of her fertility, her softness and passionate size of her breasts in her palms. She left herself completely into Inanna's arms as the seductive kiss from from her lips moved from her earlobes to her neck.

She was startled by the young nun's knocking at the room door and sat up in her bed. While looking around as if to say, "Where am I?", she realized that she was in her own room and in bed. Her mind and thoughts were faltering like a child that constantly falling down and rising up.

As she thought, "Where did I get here, and how?", she realized that she was naked. She couldn't even remember how she had taken off her clothes. She looked onto the crate that woven of sugar can which she had always put on after undressing, but it wasn't there, either. She immediately pulled out a new dress from the crate and unlocked the door by throwing her new dress from one shoulder to the other.

The young nun was waiting with a bowl and a cloth in her hand. Enheduanna welcomed her. The young nun put the bowl next to the basin that onto the long and thin table which made of date tree. She opened the curtains and the window the let the fresh air get into the room. And then she stepped back and began to wait in front of the door. Enheduanna had sat on her bed again after opening the door and was trying to wake up and remember what she had experienced last night. Was it a dream or real? After all, weren't they both the perceptions that created by her brain? What difference would it make? She was also hesitant to ask the young nun; she didn't want to cause any misunderstanding because the young nun may think that she went crazy. She stood up and walked to the basin on the table. The nun immediately came, took the bowl and poured some water to help the High Priestess wash her hands and face.

Enheduanna was planning the day in her mind while the young nun was braiding her hair which had grown below her waist. But it was the wishes of the goddess that constantly tampered with her mind; she couldn't make sense of whether it was a dream or real and she couldn't ignore it. She had to think because their demands meant a revolutionary change in the temple. Why would Inanna made such a request? Forasmuch as, the statues and altars of the gods Anu, Enlil, Nanna, Utu, Enki and Mother Goddess Nimmah had to be removed from the temple. How could she do it out of the blue? What would be the reactions of other nuns and priests? What would the people think?

Her haircare and make-up that would add more beauty to the beauty of her smooth face with herbal mixtures were completed in turn. A necklace of precious stones which was brought from distant lands for her was worn around her neck. He perfume that prepared from the essences of unique flowers was applied.

To the young nun,

''I want to see all the priests and priestesses in the Great Hall after dinner'', said she.

"With pleasure, Mother Priestess", the young nun answered and left the room.

Enheduanna walked to the window and watched the city of Ur which was stretching out before her. In the garden of the temple, women were spinning rope out of wool, sheep were being milked on one side, carpenters were chopping the trees ahead, the blacksmith was trying to fulfill his new orders, and the children were playing with each other and having fun happily. The slaves, on the other hand, were busy cleaning the garden and the temple. The land was waiting for Nowruz to spurt its fertility into the sky. The canals leading to the river was carrying the water of life to the fields. Farmers and merchants gathered in the city square and offered their goods for sale. One was selling her vegetables, the other was selling her apples. Another was behind the counter, praising his fresh zucchini and well-sweetened, ripe melons. Rows of benches are lined with beautiful and attractive ornaments for women, all types of perfume, ceramics to decorate the houses, oil lamps, amphoras and bowls made of terracotta, ivory amulets, assorted fabrics and cloths, spices that give off a fragrant smell, wheat bread fresh out of the oven recipients were waiting for its buyers.

My country is waiting for blessings, newborn children and lambs. The holy day of marriage is approaching, " she thought to herself.

She came in front of the figurine of Inanna, which was knitted from adobe and plastered with plaster and painted white, standing on the table against the wall, and knelt. She closed her eyes, joined her hands on her stomach, and began to pray as she came from within and in a tone she could hear himself.

O Inanna! You are as great as the sky, let it be known!

You're as wide as the ground, let it be known!

You're the one who roars in the land, let it be known!

You're the one who chop off the heads, let it be known!

You're the one who sweep away the corpses like a dog, let it be known!

You're the one who wins many victories, let it be known!

After she had finished and written her prayer on the clay of the dough she had taken in her hand, she got up and left her room to do her daily routines. She began to walk the corridors of the temple. While her blue eyes were watching the relief writing and paintings on the ceramic-covered adobe walls, her mind was busy thinking about how to fulfill Inanna's command. By the way, she couldn't even realize that she had come to her usual room where she was running her business. Her assistants had everything ready and were waiting for her. To Sister Amare,

"Beautiful servant of Inanna! Let's begin to take the waiting ones in order, people are impatient; they like to wait someone wait, but they hate to wait," said she and sat on her armchair.

Amare went to the hall and glanced at those who were waiting.

"You, you can come," sad she, showing the way with her hand to a girl in her twenties, slightly overweight, short, curly hair, dressed in a dress of fabric that has been used for a long time and obvious that it is outdated and the colors are fading. The girl proceeded to Enheduanna's room in quick and short steps, and when she came in front of her, she bowed slightly and greeted and sat up in bed.

One of the assistants, Nakurtum, was one of the most experienced scribes of the temple. She was a girl in her early thirties, tall, slightly overweight but beautiful and remarkable with facial contours. She always had his hair cut short to get rid of the hassle of combing every day. With her hard work, dedication to the tasks assigned, and endless energy, she became the right-hand man of Enheduanna. Her father dedicated her to the temple to become a nun when she was young. But thanks to her learning ability and quick intelligence, she was commissioned as a scribe when she became an adult girl. Since the day she arrived, Amare and Nakurtum had been both the assistants and the best friends of Enheduanna's. While Nakurtum and the other scribe were waiting with the newly prepared clay dough and reed in their hands, Nakurtum,

"Girl, what is your name?" she asked. The young girl,

" I am Ahunatum, Shulgi's daughter, " she said back. Nakurtum was writing what the girl said on clay dough.

"What do you do, Ahunatum?" she continued his questions.

"I work as a shepherd with my father."

Sitting just ten paces away, Enheduanna watched the girl from the beginning to the end as she was answering questions. It was obvious that the girl was in a bad situation; it was as if she had the mood of the person who woke up from a nightmare at night on her. Her conversation was short, sharp and tense. She was constantly rubbing the fabric of her dress with her hands. The lack of a veil on her head indicated her singlehood. From the open parts of her sandals, her calluses on her feet drew attention.

"Tell me, girl, what had brought you here, before me?"

"Sir, I have lived with my family since the day I was born, and my mother and I have always been shepherds with my father. We herded, milked, slaughtered our sheep, and gave our vow to the gods. My mother died suddenly two years ago. I've been living with my father ever since. During that time, I have matured as a summer apple, and now it's time for me to fall off the branch. By the Goddess of Inanna, I want to marry and build a family to combine my water with the water of the man I love. But my father never allows it. Last night, while I was talking in the garden with the man I wanted to marry, my father caught us. He dragged me home and beat me. He threatened to kill me. He said he wouldn't let me get married until he died. I seek refuge with you, and in the name of the gods, I ask you to judge me.''

Although the girl had the right to marry, her family's permission was required. Enheduanna thought for a while and made up her mind:

"Tomorrow is the day of sacrifice; when you come to the temple, you will bring an underage lamb as a vow with the person you are going to marry. The lamb is the vow of the one you marry. And on the night of the offering, you will go to the seclusion room of the temple, go into a relationship with a stranger, and give the price you have received to Sister Urnina to donate it to Inanna. And after Sister Urnina seals my decision, I authorize you get married. It's a paternal right for your father to beat you, but to damage to one limb of yours is to steal from you. As far as I can see, you have no loss. That's why, I don't punish your father. I, King Sargon's daughter, Enheduanna, High Priestess of the temple, that is my decision. Let the property of those who do not obey my decision be my property and his life my sacrifice!" ,she finished her speech.

Enheduanna took the written tablets in her hands and read them, sealed them both with the cylinder seal, and handed one to the girl and put the other in the wooden box. The girl who took the tablet on which the decision was written retreated back out of the room with great joy and excitement in respect and disappeared into the hallway.

Soon after, another woman Amare had brought entered the room. She was a timid woman in her forties, dirty, having messy and graying hair. She stood in front of Enheduanna. As usual, Nakurtum began to write his report on the clay tablet, identifying the person who came. Enheduanna asked why she came.

"My Holy Sister, I have been married for twenty years, and my husband is a farmer. I also work as a maid at Neti's stable. We have worked hard until today, devoted food, drinks and sacrifices to the gods. But we didn't have children. My house is quiet, my land is arid and my lap is childless. My husband wants to leave me and marry another woman. I don't want my man to flow to someone else, pull his head out of my home and put it in another home. I want a baby. I want you to add my prayer to your prayers and beg the gods for me to give me a baby. Or whatever your decision is, let it be my destiny." The woman finished her speech. Enheduanna,

"It's natural for your husband to want to marry another woman instead of you because you have no children. But once again, I invite you to pray. Tomorrow is the day of the offering; you will come to the temple, and the servants will wash, dress and prepare you. In the evening, you will offer yourself as a vow to the Great Inanna, the God of the Moon. You will share your skin and holy fruit with a man who wants to be with you on her behalf. You'll donate its price to the temple. If the man who tastes your fruit is happy, the Goddess Inanna will also be happy and give you a child. I, King Sargon's daughter, Enheduanna, the Hight Priestess of the temple, that is my decision. Let the Goddess Inanna listen to the one who obeys my decree, and let her wish be my wish, but if she does not obey, let her path be the way," said she, read the tablets, sealed them, and gave one to the woman.

After the woman had left the room, Nakurtum and Amare began to laugh quietly, looking at each other. Enheduanna wondered what they were laughing at when she saw their cheerful attitude,

"My sisters, what happened? Did I miss something?" when she asked, Nakurtum, a little shy,

"Sir, we've just wondered about the woman's husband just now, so we laughed," she replied. Still unable to satisfy her curiosity, Enheduanna asked again:

"So, what about her husband?"

''My High Priestess, I think her husband must be very good at relationship that she doesn't want to lose, this came to our mind and we couldn't help ourselves and we laughed."

"Nuns, I think today is your day. How about I put you on the seclusion if you want? You'll make both the goddess and yourself happy. Love is not in the wine that you fill in the cup and drink; it is in the hand that squeezes the juice of the grape and ferments it into the jug. Just like you don't know who loves how and what they believe, there's no way you can know."

It was optional for the nuns to go into a relationship. But Amare and Nakurtum had not gone into relationship since the day they became the assistants of High Priestess.

"Excuse Me, Mother Superior, please forgive us!",- said Nakurtum and apologized.

"There is nothing to apologize for, my nuns, whatever you do, let there be love, effort, and most importantly goodwill in it. It is the intention that grinds the wheat and makes flour, makes the flour dough, and makes the dough bread. Otherwise, that bread may be a stone burning in the ember in the baker's hand," said she and taught a small lesson.

The nuns were a little relieved when they saw Enheduanna talking with a smile. Because neither of them wanted to go into a relationship with a man they didn't want, even for the Goddess Inanna. While Enheduanna and her assistants were talking among themselves, they noticed a soldier rushing towards them through the door of the room which is open. And in silence, they watched the soldier approach them and come to the door. The soldier came in, saluting,

"My princess, a wounded man has just arrived at the city gate. A trade caravan arriving in the city of Ur was raided by a northern desert tribe a few kilometers from the city!" said he.

While Enheduanna was listening to the soldier carefully, she said to him who was gasping from running and barely understood what he said,

"Soldier, calm down, please, take a breath and go on!"

Nakurtum stood up and filled a cup with water from a jug and served it to the soldier. The soldier who drank up the water tried to calm down by controlling his breath.

"The desert tribe took the goods, women and merchants carried by the caravan with them and disappeared into the desert, Sir. The camel driver, hiding behind a sand dune in the chaos, saved himself and was able to come to our city. What do you order?"

"I got it, soldier, tell Commander Namtar to gather all the soldiers in front of the headquarters immediately and I will be right there. And tell the soldiers waiting at the temple gate to prepare my carriage!"

After the soldier had saluted, he ran through the door and disappeared into the hallway. Enraged and upset by what had happened, Enheduanna rose from her seat from and adjusted her clothes.

These people, who was living scattered and barbaric in the desert, often kept caravan routes arriving to Ur, captured the merchants by making raids and looted the caravans. Although patrols were put up on the road, this method was not always a preventive measure. The attacks worried the merchants who would come from the west and the north-west, and disrupted the commercial relations of the city.

These tribes, who dared to attack that city and looted the vineyards and gardens even before Enheduanna came to the city of Ur could not show the same courage after the new walls surrounding the city, but continued their barbarism by raiding the roads.

"Nakurtum, you come with me. Amare, my daughter, you take care of the rest."

Enheduanna and her assistant Nakurtum came out of the judgment room together, passed through the temple corridors decorated with reliefs describing his father's heroism and ascension to the throne, and came to the lower floor, and from there, to the temple door. The horses were harnessed, and one of the soldiers was waiting for them to come in the driver's seat. It didn't take them long to get to headquarters after the carriage had moved. People were drawn from the streets to relax and have lunch in their homes or dining halls in the heat of the noon. So, they were able to make their way quickly. When they arrived in front of the headquarters, the soldiers were lined up in rows of four, waiting for her with Commander Namtar. Descending from her carriage, Enheduanna came to the top of the stairs leading to the headquarters and turned to the soldiers waiting for her and said;

"Barbarian tribes who can no longer attack our city and live in the cursed deserts covered with long and parched sand right next to us, attack the trade caravans. But know that what they really want is the crops of our fertile fields, our animals, and our women who are the most beautiful on earth! What they will do at the first opportunity is to bring blood and ash to our peaceful city. That's why, it's time to teach these barbarians a lesson!"

As she began to speak in his velvety, soul-caressing beautiful voice, the soldiers who listened to him realized that Enheduanna was not only a princess and a beautiful mother superior, but also a very good orator.

"Brave men of Inanna!" she continued her speech in a loud voice, saying, "Guardians Of Ur! In the name of the goddess, in the name of my father, King Sargon, will you punish these barbarians?"

The soldiers responded to Enheduanna in chorus:

"Yes! Yes! Yes!"

Enheduanna continued, raising her hands in the air:

"So may Inanna, goddess of war, be with you! May your wrist be strong, your heart be full of courage!"

Interrupting her speech, she pointed the inscription which was written in a sizable way on the headquarters wall behind her:

"What is written here?"

The soldiers responded loudly in chorus again:

"Fight like God!"

She asked the same question again. And the soldiers responded in chorus again:

"Fight like God!"

Enheduanna could read the anger in the soldiers' eyes and the sense of revenge.

"Then, fight like God! And come back victorious!" said she and came down the stairs to the Commander Namtar.

"Assign one of your best officers with enough soldiers, commander. I don't want the same thing to happen again for a long time. Let them not touch women and children!"

"Yes, My Princess!"

As Enheduanna get in her carriage and headed for the temple, in the meantime, the chariot troops moved quickly into the desert, yellowed and scorched by the scorching heat of the sun. When Enheduanna and Nakurtum reached the temple, soldiers of Ur, athirst for war and yearning for the smell of blood, had already disappeared into the desert. At the temple, lunch was being eaten.

Although she always dined with other nuns, Enheduanna wanted to eat her meal alone with her assistants in her room today. A servant brought dishes consisting of flour soup in earthen casseroles and meaty bulgur rice with a tray. Enheduanna took the bread and kissed it, touched it to her forehead and divided it into three. They began to feed their bellies with a great appetite. At meal, Enheduanna, breaking the silence, told what she had experienced last night. She said that she would explain the situation to the other nuns and priests in the temple in the evening and order that it be done. She asked her two most trusted assistants at the temple for their opinions.

Amare and Nakurtum, who listened to the Mother Superior with their mouths open, even stopping to eat, looked at Enheduanna with greater respect and admiration. Amare spoke candidly:

"Holy priestess of Inanna, mistress of my temple. Goddess Inanna has chosen you on Earth before other gods; she has given sanctity to your sanctity, beauty to your beauty, name and honor to your reputation," bowed she and kissed the skirt of Enheduanna. Nakurtum also followed Amare in the same way and began to talk:

"Moon-faced priestess of the moon goddess Inanna, the shining and guiding star of my temple, you are the wisest of all, you know everything better than we do, " said she and continued by bowing her head forward:

"But the wish of the Great Goddess may disturb some in the temple. There may be those who do not welcome the removal of their gods, to whom they have served for years, offered vows, and given their lives from the temple. They can put you in a difficult position by provoking and confronting people against you. Let us think, also postpone the evening meeting; let's talk again among us"

24

Listening to Nakurtum carefully and seriously, Enheduanna nodded and replied:

"You're right, Sister! You inform them that the meeting has been canceled. Let's meet in my room after dinner, we'll take a boat trip and talk."

After the meal, Enheduanna toured the temple and checked the work and workers one by one. He especially devoted time to the location of the altars, one of the most important parts of the temple. It was quite important how diligently those who worked at the altar did their work and whether they failed in their respect for the gods. Because the happiness of the Gods was directly related to how much and how they were taken care of. Therefore, by gathering all those who worked at the altar; she took care of them in detail, from hand, foot cleaning to upper head cleaning. Then, she wandered the compartments in the hall where the statues of their gods were located, which were specially prepared for each God and separately. He inspected whether the hands and feet of the gods had been washed, and whether the altars were thoroughly cleaned of sacrificial blood.

Then, she moved to the side where the temple school was located. This school, where the smartest and brightest children of Ur learned literacy and government affairs, was the place where Enheduanna cared most. It consisted of three separate sections: Children who learn to read and write in the first part move on to the second part and undergo a more serious education; they studied history, geography, religious knowledge, astronomy, mathematics and music. The third part was the final stage; students were taking courses on state administration and bureaucracy at this stage.

It was here that the future rulers and temple employees grew up. Children crouched on the floor in rows of three, with clay batters and reed pens in their hands, were busy writing samples given by their teachers. She glanced at each of their tablets one by one by walking among them. She sometimes corrected the mistakes she saw, gave some advice. She accompanied several students by crouching, and showed her affection by patting their heads. When she realized that everything was fine by looking at the second and third sections through the door, she moved to the chamber of the priest who was in charge of the temple school.

The Priest Ahikibani, who was in charge of the temple school, was also in charge of the observance. He gave the impression of being serious and responsible with his long height, his squinted eyes that tired of reading a lot under his thick eyebrows, his wide and nervous face. Priest Ahikibani, an intellectual person who devoted his life to his students and reading at school, stood up and saluted when he saw Enheduanna. In a sign of deep respect, he joined his hands above his belly and gently bowed his head down. Although he was over fifty years old, his voice sounded like that of a young man in his thirties:

"Welcome, my Mother Superior!"after he said, he presented his place to Enheduanna.

"I will not stay long, Priest Ahikibani, I visited the school and also wanted to visit you on my way back."

"Your grace, Sir.''

"I will send you hymns that I have written for you to teach as a lesson to the students in the second section and duplicate by writing. I want you to deal with this."

"Yes, Mother Superior!" said Priest Ahikibani, and then, he bowed his head again and offered his approval and respect to her.

After leaving the school, Enheduanna disappeared inside the other corridors of the temple for her routine controls. It was only her body walking with her thoughts spiralling in her mind. She was lost in thoughts and she even wasn't aware of where she was going.

Because of her faith, she was also afraid to question the goddess's wish. But from the edge of her mind, the question "Why did she want that?" was gnawing her mind. It was a question that she was too afraid to express. But also, as one of the best representatives of the dream interpretation tradition that her ancestors had shaped with their experiences for thousands of years, she was also conscious of what her own dream meant. Although she didn't want to admit it, her brain was actually answering the question in her head. From the tablets that were the legacy of her ancestors, she had read about the struggle and test of her ancient people with the gods. She had witnessed not only the struggle of her Sumerian ancestors, but also the struggle of the gods with each other. The sentence of her teacher, Aya, who was deliberately murdered by someone unknown, came to her mind: *"Knowledge is light, and light takes you from darkness to light,"* said she once. As long as she learned, her horizon had broaden and she had begun to find herself in a different intellectual world. Ambition and power were not just a goal or a dream that people chased. Gods and goddesses had struggled and fought for the same things. Maybe, this war was still going on.

Suddenly, Gilgamesh came to her mind who cut off the head of Humbaba, the guardian of the cedar forests where the gods lived, whose voice was thunder and whose breath is fire. For his people, perhaps for himself, he had declared war not on Humbaba, but on god Enlil, and wrote the epic of humanity's victory over the gods. Eventually, Enlil would be defeated. Not only Enlil, but evil would also lose with him. Wasn't this also the story that humanity could never become a God?

She had also heard that in a country in the west where dark-skinned people lived, they worshipped their kings as The God. But she never saw it. She couldn't figure out whether kings were becoming gods, or gods were becoming kings; eventually they were dying. But do the gods die? Gilgamesh could not become a God and find eternity, and tasted death at the end that life had drawn for him. Or could it be the gate of eternity, not death? Were all the gods once human and death paved the way for them to divinity? Gilgamesh had got eternal life and power, but could not achieve divinity after death. Maybe he was cursed, maybe he paid for his rebellion, who knows?

Her beloved goddess, to whom she dedicated her life and body, in fact, no longer wanted war with what she wanted from herself. He did not want blood to be shed, everything to turn into chaos as before, and mankind try to be destroyed by a flood as Enlil did. What Inanna wanted was a quiet revolution. And she wanted that revolution to be in the heart and brain of mankind, where all the gods lived and to be lived. If Enheduanna, as the chosen man, could achieve this, she was sure that Inanna, the goddess of all gods, the moon, fertility and war, would do the rest.

After all, why was she alive? Hadn't she dedicated everything, his life, his blood, his body to Inanna when she stepped into the girlhood? Everything was for her. Wasn't this temple built for her, too? What was necessary had to be done? Just as the river continues to flow despite all the channels and dams built, no matter how long humanity tries to live, it is defeated by a snake bite, every born dies one day, and if someone else is born in its place, what should have happened would definitely happen!

Besides, what could the meaning of the seas, mountains, endless sky and the earth decorated with a thousand kinds of plants be if there were no human beings? Wasn't it Inanna who made the continuation of the generation, gave life to nature by springing life from the soil, gave lamb to sheep and daughter to mankind? What if the others exist without Inanna? Wasn't man tested by what he believed?

As thoughts, questions and answers revolved around his mind like a Ferris wheel which children play with, she suddenly felt to urge to pray. She came before the altar of Inanna, and kneeling down, in a voice that all the priests and nuns could hear, the sentences born into her began to pour out of his plump and moist lips:

In the mountains where you are not worshipped, plants are cursed.

You're the one who turned the greatness of everything to ashes.

Rivers shed bloody tears for you,

And people can not find water to drink.

The arms of the mountains become dam for you with their own harmony.

Healthy young men,

Line up before you with their own harmony.

Dancing city is filled with storms,

Makes the young men captive by throwing them in front of you.

30

During the communal meal after the temple work that continued throughout the day, she examined the faces of each nun and Priest one by one from one end of the tables to the other. All of them had the peace and fatigue of doing their daily duties properly on their faces. Well, tomorrow there will be the same fatigue on those faces, but will she be able to see peace?

A day later, as it was the day of the vow, there would be no night rite. The one who finished his/her meal could freely do whatever he/she wanted. Anyone could go to the city, anyone could retreat to their room and rest, anyone could go to taverns who wanted to drink and have fun, drink beer and have fun until later in the night, and could make love to whomever they wanted and wherever they wanted...Except for Enheduanna.

As everyone was dispersing, Amare went to Belanum, one of the veteran priests of the temple, and began to speak:

"Dear priest, I want to ask you something."

The priest pointed to one of the dining tables for her to sit, nodding gladly. Amare, looking left and right to check if anyone is there,

"Priest Belanum, what does it mean dream of the goddess and talk to her?" asked she.

The priest was surprised by this question. Raising his tired head and his eyes wide open,

"Sister Amare, you are blessed!" said he and got up from the wooden stool where he was sitting on, bent down and kissed Amare's feet.

Amare, who was surprised at what to do in the face of this unexpected move, stood up in surprise and reacted in an ashamed way:

"Oh, Sir, what are you doing?"

She grabbed Belanum, the old priest, by the arms and lifted him up and put him back on his stool. Belanum kept talking:

"Well, did the Goddess say or make a request to you?"

Amare didn't know what to say. She responded quickly and cursory, missing her eyes from the priest:

"I don't remember exactly right now, Father Belanum."

The priest joined his hands on his chest, bowing his head with deep respect and humility:

"No creature or God can enter the dream of a person disguised as Inanna, my beautiful girl. If you have seen Inanna, she is definitely Inanna, and it means that she has blessed you. For this, you must make a vow that Inanna might want. You need to express your gratitude and pray," said he.

Amare asked this conversation to stay between them, thanked him and then went to the bath for the evening decontamination.

After the meal, the silence that suffocated the temple was disrupted by the footsteps of the two nuns. After Amare and Nakurtum had done their evening self care, they came to Enheduanna's room. The High Priestess, who was waiting for them, was busy writing on the tablets the new prayers that passed through her mind and said throughout the day. When her guests arrived, she let them in. After she had finished writing her prayers, they arrived at the entrance under the flickering and pale light of oil lamps hanging on the wall in the darkened temple corridors and dancing on the wall in the gentle breeze. Although the sun had set, it was not still dark. The sun which disappeared in the west was reminding people that they should go to their homes by building its red lights like a wall between it and the darkness. The stars began to show themselves and were almost competing with each other to escape and become visible again behind sparse clouds. The evening star, on the other hand, took its place on the horizon like the forerunner and the guard of the night, wrapped into the dark spike color, gazing at the earth, started to glitter as if "I'm here!" between the darkness and red. As spring approached, the cold began to lose its effect, and it began to let the hot air from its broken places to the Sumerian lands. With the disappearing sunlight, the temperature also decreased, it became a coolness that did not feel cold, but felt itself. City workers went forward with long torches in their hands, lighting oil lamps in the streets, and as they went forward, the lightness also spread through the city, breaking the darkness with them.

Enheduanna and her assistants walked along the streets step by step, passing by the whitewashed houses line up side by side, inspecting the city without breaking the silence between them. As people who had finished their work made their way to their homes in a hurry, the voices of children and sellers in the streets of Ur left their place to the sounds of sandals on the stone floor. The city was still alive, but this liveliness was about to surrender to the fatigue left over from the day. Soon, Ur would turn into a city as quiet as a desert, as desolated as a cemetery, and resembling death. They came to the port, which is next to the military headquarters, with calm steps and keeping their silence. The ten-meter-long boat with a single sail, made of cedar wood, which his father had allocated to her, was anchored in this harbor, the shallowest part of the river. The keel at the end of the boat curved upwards and was rising to a man's height. At the top of it, a relief lion's head stood like a guard protecting the ship. For its square-shaped and densely woven sail couldn't be adjusted against the wind, it had to be either wait or be rowed by four oarsmen to carry it forward. At the back, there was a protocol place resembling a fountain, which was built high and covered with leather. This was the area where Enheduanna or the royal person would sit, sleep, and eat during the voyage. Just behind this part was the helmsman's section.

After commanding the soldiers waiting at the port entrance to prepare her boat, Enheduanna in the front and her assistants behind her got on the boat one by one. They moved into the protocol area at the stern and sat down.

Fishing boats that didn't sail into the river were lined up around the port. A warship was anchored at the entrance of the port, ready for an extraordinary situation to arise, waiting with its dreadful appearance and weapons. The merchant ships that arrived to the city were also anchored on the opposite shore, which was reserved for them. They couldn't take their eyes off the city, which descended to the shore from where the temple was. The light glided out of the streets and houses flashed like fireflies and circled the darkened walls around the city. The sounds of grasshoppers and frogs around the river also accompanied this light. On the huge two-legged-bridge made of large stone blocks connecting the city across the river, the soldiers kept their watch by going back and forth. For security reasons, the soldiers on the bridge, which was not illuminated in the evening, were barely noticeable in the reflected light of the city, like the shadows of leaves moving in the wind. They felt the presence of moisture better in every breath they inhaled when compared to the temple. The unique smell of seaweed of the river itself was dominated in the air. During the time they spent waiting for the officers, they forgot all the tiredness of the day, refreshed their conscious and became vigorous. The helmsman's question broke the silence between them:

"Where would you like to go, My Princess?"

Enheduanna didn't know where to go for sightseeing as she did not sail very often. She only used the boat once a month while going to her brother, who was stationed in Uruk. Turning undecidedly to the helmsman,

"Take us to the most beautiful places we can go and see, soldier", said she.

The slaves who were going to row were seated, sailed, and the boat began to sail to the south in darkness, with four soldiers in charge of security positioned at the back. It was only the sounds of grasshoppers and frogs that continued to accompany them as the lights of the city gradually faded behind them. The sounds that the oars made while breaking the water were also mixed into these sounds. The dangerous, ferocious, and quiet owners of the waters were not in sight yet. The stars that shone upon them with their all splendor and illuminated the night poured down their splendor like a rain of light. The passengers were silent, but nature was talking. The earth and the sky commemorated Inanna in their own language, and dedicated their most beautiful poems to her with their own music. The stars circulated around the pole star like dancer girls performing their most agile moves, and the darkness was home to the stars, grateful to the sunset for allowing it. Entering a completely different mood in the face of the unique landscape of nature, Enheduanna broke the silence with her velvety voice:

"How neat and beautiful everything is! Life has returned to itself. My Lord Inanna has ended thousands of years of revenge and wars. Love and beauty won when she dominated everything. Peace and life have come to the universe," said she and turned her attention to the nuns.

While the light from the end of the ship illuminated part of the nuns' faces, the other part was shaded like bottom of an oil lamp. They turned their attention to the Princess, too. Enheduanna continued:

"I had read it on the tablets in The Palace Library in metropolis. They were very old tablets. According to the librarian, it was at least a few thousand years old. It was understood that it was quite old because the writings on it was about to be erased. It was obvious that it yielded to time, beginning the edges of it crumble and fall off. There were older ones than that tablet, telling the stories of our ancient ancestors. There was a city in the north called Anu, and when our ancestors first settled there, their leader named it Anu. Later, Anu, the leader of our ancestors, had many children. When these children grew up, they left Anu and emigrated. Some are scattered to the East, some to the west or South, and some to the North. These are the Anunnaki. The children of Anu, our ancestors, who scattered to all directions and carried our generation and custom to the places they went."

Nakurtum was shocked, realizing the gap between what Enheduanna had told to her and what she had learned so far. She heard it for the first time in her life. She also did not read it. She felt the need to ask what was stuck in her mind from his astonishment, facial expressions and tone of voice clearly, and asked her question, taking the advantage of Enheduanna's breathing:

"But, sir, they have always told us about the Anunnaki as our gods. But you say they were the children of our first ancestors, that is, human beings, just like us."

Enheduanna looked at Nakurtum smiling:

"I understand your curiosity and haste, my sister, and I will tell you now. These tablets were under special protection, but I had the opportunity to read some of them. The tablets I talked about were written by an abbot named Ennugi. Once upon a time, our ancestors used to believe in one God. That God used to be everywhere, just like the air we breathed. It used to be both inside and outside of us. It used to be the source of life. Then, our ancestors cut that unique God into pieces like cheese slices and shaped it as they wanted. One became the God of Lightning, the other became the God of Rain, and another became the God of the Sun. And they gave the names of our ancestors, our leaders, to the gods so that they would not be forgotten, but remembered with respect. When I combined what I was taught with what I read on these tablets, I loved Inanna more and dedicated myself to her. At our meeting with Inanna, I realized that my efforts and thoughts over the years were not in vain. What I knew until then had made me doubt it, but now I'm sure," said she and fell into silence for a while.

Then she took her little lyre out of the cupboard next to him; she touched his strings with her thin and long, cotton-soft fingers. She began to recite a prayer accompanied by unique music that embellished with delicate notes, making the human's hair stand on end, and touching:

Inanna,
Who knows what is in our heart and the future,
Who sees everything with our eyes,
Who hears everything with our ears,
You're the sun rising against the night,
You're the rising against the day,
You're my thinking mind,
You're my pen that writes,
You're the river that gives life to my country,
Like the moon changing every day
You're the one who changed the Earth,
You're the only owner of all beauty.

Sister Amare and Nakurtum, with the influence of the environment they were in, passed through them along with the poem of Enheduanna. Nakurtum thought about what she had lost and felt worried, remembering that although she had given her years to the temple as a clergyman, she had never experienced such a moment. She had supposed that faith could only be lived in the temple, and the gods could only be reached in the temple. But in the peaceful environment she was now in, under the stars, she had found Inanna on the deck of a boat she didn't know where it was going. She breathed, and let it out. She breathed again and let it out again. Yeah, that was awesome! God was everywhere, like the air she inhaled. She was breathing and integrating with God. Inanna breathed life into her lungs. She couldn't control the enthusiasm in him,

"This is awesome, Sir, it's wonderful, thank you very much!" said she, hugged and kissed Enheduanna's hands. Enheduanna who began to caress her hair by lowering the scarf over Nakurtum's head on her shoulder

"Tell me sister, tell me about your feelings and thoughts you've lived," said she.

Nakurtum sat up slightly and knelt down above the deck.

"I felt Inanna, Sir! I felt her inside of me, next to me. I realized it was her with every breath I took; I can't explain it, Sir! Until my age, I thought I could only find gods in temples, their homes. It wasn't so, it wasn't so, Sir! She's here now, even inside of me ..."

She couldn't keep the tears flowing from her eyes. Her joy and sadness, mixed like water and salt, were flowing from her eyes in drops. The peace that covered her silenced even the beating of her heart. Enheduanna was happy that the emotions she wanted to live and let live dominated Nakurtum and began to speak in a way that supported her:

"Yes, my sister, I experienced what you are going through years ago, when I was only 14, sitting alone in my room thinking. I still live. I realized that the teachings had locked my mind when my thoughts began to open those locks. Mind exists in every living being, but it is the ability to think that develops and differentiates people."

She interrupted her speech when she realized that the lieutenant, who was in charge of the soldiers boarded the ship for their safety, was coming to them. The lieutenant was a tall young man with his hair growing up to his neck and mixed with his beard. His eyes under his thick eyebrows, tilted in the shape of an arch and next to his huge nose, were so small that it was necessary to look carefully to notice. The lieutenant calmly approached and saluted them,

"I beg your pardon, Sir. I'm Lieutenant Eluti. I inadvertently overheard your words. Let me ask you something."

Enheduanna felt uneasy, realizing that they were not being cautious while talking to the nuns. Their inner state made them forget that they were not alone. She thought she should have been more careful. She remembered the day when her teacher Aya, who taught her to use her mind and think, introduced her to the library and made it her favorite place, was found her lifeless body at the foot of the palace wall. They said she fell out the window. But Enheduanna never believed it. Looking at the lieutenant's vague face in the dark,

"Here you are, Lieutenant, permission is yours." She reluctantly gave permission and ordered the helmsman to return.

She hoped the lieutenant hadn't been offended with what was being talked, or that he hadn't understood much. She knew that one of the hardest things in life was to change people's minds. The last thing she wanted right now was to get herself into a trouble that dangerous as well as exhausting. She had never seen one side won an intellectual debate. Their unwilling acceptance was not because they agreed, but because of their fears. Although this fear brought acceptance, it then fed hostility. When she gave the lieutenant permission, she heard the other soldiers at the end of the ship giggling among them. She couldn't hear what it was about because the sounds of frogs and grasshoppers drowned out the hoarse voices of soldiers.

"You said that our ancestors believed in one God at first, but then divided God into slices like cheese and made each of them the God of another power. So, if these powers were not gods, what are they, sir? Lightning, for example? Or the wind..."

"Can't all these powers be God himself, Lieutenant?"

Enheduanna wanted to answer the question with another question and understand what the lieutenant was thinking.

"So, the one who makes the lightning strike, the one who makes the wind blow, the one who makes the rain fall... Isn't it all the same God himself?"

It was clear that the lieutenant was confused and had difficulty understanding something. His questions were those of a man seeking answers to the questions in his mind rather than a sense of hostility. His astonishment showed curiosity and ignorance.

"Why not, Lieutenant?"

Asking another question after the question, Enheduanna planned to take control and solve the Lieutenant. The lieutenant's silence and bewilderment showed that he had no idea about it. She didn't want to make everything boring by waiting any longer.

"When you, lieutenant, think of taking the apple on the table, you do it with your hand, not with your mind, don't you? Or, when you hear a sound, you see it with your eyes when you look at it, wondering where this sound comes from. Don't your hands, your feet, your mind, your eyes, and all your limbs make you as one and only part of your existence and life?"

The lieutenant was confused. What Enheduanna said sounded so alien and contradictory that what she knew and heard was at war in his mind. What the Princess had said were not the ideas that could be disregarded.

"Think like this; can't every power we experience in life also be a part and limb of Goddess Inanna's vital existence? Would it be ridiculous for him to rule the world and everything in it that way?"

The lieutenant thought for a while. He realized that he couldn't get out of these thoughts, which were meaningful but difficult to accept right now.

"So, why Inanna? Can't she be the God Enki or Enlil himself?"

That was the question that Enheduanna didn't want to be asked. How could she explain her own experience with Inanna to a soldier she never knew, and was unsure whether to trust or not?

"Most people use the gods in the sky as they please. But I chose only Inanna. And I chose to serve only her.

I call her Inanna, Lieutenant, you can call her Enki or by another name. What matters is not what her name is, but who he is."

The answer sounded reasonable to Lieutenant. After all, it didn't matter what his name was. The important thing was that it existed. The Elamites could call the fruit that they called apples something else. But it didn't change the taste, appearance or shape of the apple.

"Thank you, sir. I'm sorry for disturbing you," said he, saluted and turned to the other soldiers with complicated thoughts in his head. He also found them discussing the topics which he had discussed with The Princess among themselves.

When Enheduanna, wondering about Amare who had been silent for a long time, looked at her, she saw that she had fallen asleep where she was sitting with her head down, and smiled. Realizing the situation, when Nakurtum nudges Amare with his elbow, the nun suddenly startled saying "No, no!" and came to herself.

The effect of the last dream she had seen continued when she woke up. It was clear from her eyes that she had trouble in understanding where she was when she opened her eyes. It didn't take her long to realize.

"Excuse Me, Mother Superior! I took a nap from exhaustion."

It was obvious that she was embarrassed by his facial expressions and tone of voice. Her neck was stiff because it fell forward. She tried to relax by tilting it slightly to the right and left. She hadn't even realized how long she'd been asleep. And she also was ashamed to ask. The last thing she remembered was that Enheduanna was talking about a tablet in the library.

"Is this your first time on the boat, Sister Amare?"

The nun still couldn't get over the stupor of sleep.

"Yes, sir, it's my first time riding. As a matter of fact, I felt nauseous a little at first, but I got used to it."

"I fell asleep when I first got on, Sister, don't be shy. As the ship swings in the water like the cradle of small children, you get to sleep, don't you?" said she and gave a little laugh. It was followed by Nakurtum's titter.

As Enheduanna and the nuns were talking among themselves, the argument of the soldiers at the front of the boat began to change dimension. Their stormy speeches and threatening words came to Enheduanna's ears. Before long, oral discussion was replaced by pushing and arguing. Enheduanna and the nuns could see very clearly what was going on under the boat's lantern. One of the soldiers made a move towards the lieutenant with a dagger in his hand, shouting "infidel", and at that moment the Lieutenant limberly dodged and made the attack failed. Then, he landed a punch on the back of the soldier's neck. Seeing this, one of the other soldiers threw his fist towards the Lieutenant, but his hand remained in the air with the intervention of the other soldier standing next to the Lieutenant. Taking advantage of the situation, the Lieutenant threw a hard punch to the stomach of the soldier who attacked him. The soldier who doubled up in two by the blow he felt, fell next to the other soldier who was lying unconscious on the floor with a hard blow to the back of his neck.

Worried about what was going on, the nuns cuddled Enheduanna, watching the soldiers with fearful eyes. When Enheduanna saw that everything had calmed down, she got up and went to the Lieutenant.

"For God's sake, what happened here, Lieutenant, what is it you can't share? "

"My Princess, we were talking to these two soldiers about the gods. But after a while, they crossed the line of nurture and started swearing at you. I warned them, but this time they started insulting the Goddess Inanna. I said that they would give an account to the major when we got back to headquarters. They attacked me, and I had to protect myself."

"I hope you were not injured. I'm sorry, tonight shouldn't have ended like this. But it's my fault. I had to think about who I should get on the boat with. I'll do so next time. Tie up these soldiers and tell Commander Namtar that they have been arrested on my orders. I'll give the necessary instructions tomorrow."

The Lieutenant didn't like the idea of the soldiers being arrested.

"My Princess, I think arresting is not a good idea. Anyone who opposes me and insults you as their commander tonight can do more tomorrow. I personally wouldn't ask them to talk nonsense at headquarters."

Enheduanna took her eyes off the Lieutenant's face and turned them towards the city of Ur, which was beginning to shine ahead, thoughtfully,

"What do you think, Lieutenant?" asked she.

The Lieutenant caught the other soldier's eye next to him for a while, and he answered without waiting, as if he had already made up his mind. His speech was clear:

"They must die, My Princess!"

Enheduanna didn't have many options. He also liked the Lieutenant's determination and courage.

"I leave it to you, Lieutenant, you'll do the necessary!" said she and turned to the nuns and they began to wait in silence for what more would happen and return to city of Ur.

The Lieutenant and the soldier next to him held the soldiers, who were lying unconscious on the ground, by their hands and feet one by one, and left them into the waters of the river. There was a sudden sensation of movement around the boat. The crocodiles waiting for their hunting in the secluded and shallow places of the river snatched the bodies thrown into the water with their wide and terrifying mouths and pulled them under the water. They shook them a few times, took them back to the surface of the water between their long noses, and dived into the depths of the the river with a sudden movement again. It didn't take long, the crocodiles' fluttering in the water was over, and the river turned back to its previous silence. The people on the boat froze where they were. Their faces turned white as if their blood had been drawn from their bodies. The chilling and deadly silence was broken as the helmsman called out to the rowers:

"Hang on to the oars!"

Although they could not see in the dark, they could imagine that the water turned crimson. Enheduanna didn't even think that the Lieutenant had planned such an end for the men. Thankfully they were unconscious and died without pain, he thought.

It was night until they came to the temple and went up to Enheduanna's room. Although they were not tired, the tragedy they experienced had made them nervous. They all sat on couches set in the corner of the room. Enheduanna gave each a sugar cane stick so that they could drink and a large glazed pot full of beer.

They drank their beer without talking for a long time, tried to think and calm down. They all had the idea of what had happened in the evening and what they should do tomorrow. Enheduanna asked the question two nuns expected:

"What are we going to do now?"

Both nuns took turns telling their own ideas, explained what would be better for them to do and how. Enheduanna listened attentively to both of them. While listening, she tried to combine the stories of both nuns by fictionalizing them in her head and come up with a single plan. Last talking Amare,

"My High Priestess, hoping that you will allow me, after dinner today, I asked to the priest Belanum, the dream interpreter of the temple, what it meant to see and talk to the Goddess Inanna in a dream. You know he's one of the oldest priests of this temple. He has been doing this job in the temple for sixty years. He said that no living being and god could enter a person's dream under the guise of Inanna, and the person he entered into his dream meant that he/she is blessed by her. In that case, it was necessary to make a vow Inanna would want and pray," said he and as the priest Belanum had done to her, she stood up, bowed before Enheduanna and kissed her feet.

Then Nakurtum repeated the same thing, too. Enheduanna stroked the heads of both nuns.

"I know, my beautiful Amare, remember that I am also a dream interpreter. Dreams are the liberation of the human soul from the body it is trapped in, freedom, the purest guide," said she and smiled.

Both nuns took their seats again. Enheduanna continued:

49

" Let's prepare our plan tonight, I will say my best prayer for her, and Amare, you will go into solitude in the name of Inanna instead of me. I will give you the price," said she and took a sip of her beer.

As they were drinking their beers, Enheduanna explained the plan she had made in her mind to the smallest detail. She said who would take on what duty. She then washed her hands and arms with the water in the bowl on the table. She tidied her cloak on her head, shook off the dust on her dress. Assistant nuns also followed Enheduanna. They all knelt before the statue of Goddess Inanna in front of the wall and began to pray aloud.

Enheduanna got up from her crouch, went to her bed and stripped off her dress. She lay down on the bed naked. Her breasts as fresh and alive as a newly ripened fruit showed that two beauties could stand together so harmoniously with the vibration they gave to every movement, dispelled lust, waited to be decked out. Her magnificently beautiful hips were opened, with lines that would make even her creator jealous, and spread in aesthetics that even the best sculptors could not create. Her thin and fragile belly was swaying on the bed like a boat on the waves. It was as if love had settle down on the earth and found its meaning in Enheduanna's body.

She had felt relaxed slightly. She let her body ease in one of her deepest sleep.

The nuns watching the Holy Sister Enheduanna's beauty and drinking their beers for a time, lay on the sofa and fell asleep hugging each other.

Amare secluding herself on behalf of Enheduanna was to serve herself as an offer to Inanna. Those who didn't want to seclude themselves would seclude the nuns paying the charge. Seclusion is the coupling ceremony of Sumerian women having a deep trouble that they couldn't overcome, reaping less productions, having infertile sheep or cows, having less abundance at home, being unable to have any children or their offerings not accepted by the other Gods in a small amount of charge. The mor pleased and happier the man with the making love was, the more pleased the Goddess Inanna were. Before this offering ceremony, the temple servicers would wash, clean, adorn and help the offering woman wear good clothes and take to the seclusion room. The woman waited here for the man who would couple with her. After making love, she used to donate this charge to the temple for her offering. The temple servicer used to get this charge and register the donation date and the donor on the tablets. Then the woman used to go her home peacefully and securely thinking that her pray would be accepted. This was also the way to thank and appreciation to the Goddess Inanna. Inanna was the God of love and blessings. It was not a shameful behaviour for a woman to offer herself in this way, it was a holy duty however. For this reason, the secluded nuns were also called as Holy Whores.

In every coupling, the coupling of Inana and Dumuzi was imitated to make the country more blessed because sexuality and fertility represented the abundance. Dumuzi was released each spring-Nowruz from the underground he was captivated and his sister replaced him. Dumuzi was re-married Inanna everytime he was released and coupled with her. This coupling was the encounter of the summer and the winter. The winter represented the male and the summer represented the female. The winter fertilized the spring and the land started producing crop and tree producing fruit. The nature started coming back to life. Sumerians applying this ritual symbolically hoped that they would have more fertile lands, breeding animals and healthy children. This ritual was very important for Sumerians because their livings were completely based on agriculture and husbandry. Lands without crops, infertility and animals unable to breed meant hunger for them.

They woke up early in the morning due to the noise of the workers in the temple before the servant young nun came. Amare feeling very shy wore her clothes at once and went out greeting Enheduanna nodding without saying anything. Nakurtum stood up and and sat on the bed near Enheduanna.

"You, the high Priestess are the living form of the Goddess Inanna on the earth. I love you and adore you." said she and kissed her neck inhaling her odour. She left the room greeting her.

What Nakurtum had said pleased Enheduanna very much. Maybe, Nakurtum had told her what she was shy to express on her own.

She sat up on her bed before the young nun came and wore her clothes made of two pieces. She went to bath hurriedly to wash herself. When she entered the bath, Amare and Nakurtum were busy with washing themselves. She smiled teasing when she saw them,

"My daughters have been here, too" said she and started washing sitting on a stone.

Being clean was a very important feature of Sumerians remaining from their ancestors. Bathing must have certainly been performed especially after the coupling otherwise, they would make everywhere they touched and stepped on infertile.

The temple started getting busier when the sun was rising slowly in the early hours of the morning. People were coming to the temple slowly to serve their offerings to the Gods and pray. The ones who didn't offer anything were waiting impatiently and curiously for the night to join the supper, drink the wonderful beers that the temple priests had prepared with a great care, listen to soft music played by the player nuns using drums and lyres, watch the dances of the dancer nuns with their sexy and lithe bodies and make love with them. Everything must have been wonderful today. People must have been happy and this happiness must make the Gods happy, too.-, for this reason, the priests and priestesses were working more than before.

The priests were getting the sacrifices for their owners and taking to the altars. They had already started sacrificing the first ones in the altars.

The priests were sacrificing the animals gently and without giving them pain after they had whispered the prays of their owners into their right ears and letting the blood into the altar before the statuette of the God. The blood of the sacrificed animal meant life and it was believed that the offered God had been given life when the blood of the sacrifice had been taken out. After the blood was fully dropped from the sacrifice, the priest cut them into pieces, sent to the kitchen of the temple after the right legs and kidneys were cooked in bansurs to serve the Gods and the rest was given to their owners. On the opposite wall of the hall in which the sacrifice was made and the blood was dropped, a rule like, order, required by a very old belief was read:

"Sheep is a protection of humanity, humans must sacrifice a sheep for their lives, a sheep for a human."

The offers of the people who wanted to do but couldn't bring them on time, but brought later had been sacrificed by the priest not as an offer but an alms. As a punishment, they were not given the pieces of the saduk due to delay and the whole piece was served the God.

Not only the animals were served as an offer. Those who wish could offer fruit, vegetable or cereal. They were put into the same bansur after cooking and prepared for the feast of the Gods.

While Amare and Nakurtum got around to check the workers, Enheduanna went to the study room to prepare the pray she would read for the Goddess Inanna before the supper and write it on the tablet. She sat on the sofa in front of the window. She closed her eyes after getting her reed pencil and soft hair tablet. She imagined herself kneeling before Inanna bending her head and respecting. She spoke to Inanna in her heart:

"Mother of mothers! the Goddess of the Gods! high of the highs, strengthen my mind and tongue. Make me think like you and speak on your behalf."

It didn't take too long, her pray had been accepted and the necessary power had been reached her. She started writing on the tablet whatever came to her mind:

"I am the high priestess, Enheduanna!
You are the high of the highs, Inanna!
Your tenderly smile
Is the cause of our joy!
Your soft glance is our sun
You are the taste of our bread
And the cause of our loves!
You are the highest love and freedom!
No matter how I feel!
I can't express you neither on the ground nor in the sky
My temple is your heart full of love!
Shed lights over us and your blessings!
Accept our offers be your sacrifice
And the blood be your life!
Our loving bodies be yours
And the pleasures be your happiness
The songs playing for you!
All the dances are for you!
All the holy water running for you!
This temple and the humans for you!

Live long to make us survive
Be happy to make us happy!
Accept us up to your throne tonight
Or join us please, Inanna!

Enheduanna had passed away when she was writing her pray. She had a few drops down on her cheeks and fell on the tablet she was writing on. She couldn't see ahead due to the fog before her eyes. She felt as if she were in a thick cloud. She sat her reed pencil and the hair tablet aside. She closed her eyes again leaning back. She felt that her soul rose out of her body. She could see herself sitting down when she looked down from high above. She rose more. She saw her temple, the people running around and working in it, the cultivated farms, the channels through which the life water ran and the shepherds feeding their animals. She was so free and above as a bird. She wanted to dance swaying in the air like birds and clapping her hands like fluttering. The higher she rose, the smaller the things on the ground became. She felt that she was in a different world in her own body. A type of peace that she hadn't felt before surrounded her completely. She tried to feel that moment closing her eyes.

She dreamed of the Goddess Inanna, her perfect beauty and absolute existence. She thought of her magnificence that the Gods An, Enlil and Enki donated her with their power to the Goddess. She felt relieved thinking of the only and almighty creator which showed her existence with the signs on the earth. Inanna was everywhere. She was in the reeds used to build houses and cities. When the reed turned into a pencil, she was in it to make use of the pencil properly and usefully. She was in the cereal to provide food for temples, the bread appeasing the hunger, the tool plowing the farm and everything necessary for life.

The love for Inanna was different from the ones of her ancestors. It was similar to choose Inanna accepting the others non existing rather than forming and personating the Gods like her ancestors according to their tastes. It should have been in this way, otherwise, why did the other Gods left their power to Inanna? She was the most powerful and the only one any more. The existence of others had been lost in Inanna's unity. Why shouldn't the things her ancestors wrote on their tablets and had already been forgotten be true?

Inanna was not only everywhere but also existed always. She drops on the ground in the rain drops blessing the land and took the first place in the wars. She implied the waking life with the star visible during the sun rise and handle the nights with the stars visible during the sun set. She was the life source existing in the blood in her veins helping her survive. She was hope for the future in every newly born child.

She passed another emotional and different world from her imaginary and thoughtful world she was currently in when Inanna whispered. She couldn't see the Goddess. She couldn't dream her, either but Inanna's soft heart beating voice shaking her heart and taking her away was easing her ears. Inanna was speaking to her.

My father presented me the skies!
He presented the earth,
I am Inanna!
The kingdom he presented
The way he made me queen
He taught me to struggle in the war!
He taught to defeat!
The flood he presented
The storm he presented
The sky is the stone he helped me wear
The earth is the sandals he helped me wear
the holy cloth surrounding me
and it was the stick he handed
The Gods are sparrows and I am a hawk!

She startled and opened her eyes when she heard Nakurtum's voice calling her: "My lady, my lady, are you ok?"

She was surprised. She tried to feel conscious for a time. She sat up on the bed and crossed her legs. She fingered her hair backward. She rubbed her eyes. Firstly, she looked through the window. When the light dazed her eyes, she turned her eyes to Nakurtum. What she had been through was so real that she was sure she wasn't dreaming. She hadn't gone mad, either. She stopped and inhaled a few deep breathes.

""Please, bring me a cup of water, Nakurtum." she said.

The nun stood up at once and filled the pitcher with water on the table and brought it to Enheduanna. Enheduanna stretched the cup back to her after she drank. While getting the cup, she asked:

"Are you fine, lady. I have called and poked you so much but you haven't moved even. I thought that you had died instantly. I have felt shaken of fear."

"I am fine, dear nun, I am fine. How can you know that we are living? Maybe, we all are dead and in a deep sleep. Who can know about it?"

"You look so pale as limestone. You don't look fine. Shall I call one of the healer nuns?"

"I don't need any healer, dear nun. I am fine. I think you tired me much yesterday." she said smiling.

Nakurtum smiled when she saw that Enheduanna had smiled. She bent down her head and remembered why she had come here.

"My dear Holy Sister, as we spoke yesterday, I called the city guard Namtar. He is waiting for you in the hall. If you want, I can send him back. He could come in the evening."

"The evening is too late, dear nun. You know there are celebrations in the evening. WE must be with the public otherwise, we could be misunderstood."

"You are right, my lady. Let me call him and you speak with him as soon as possible."

Nakurtum got out of the room, went to the hall and invited the waiting, city guard Namtar. He was one of the most obedient and brave commanders of the king Sargon. He had worked under the orders of the former king Ur Zababa for many years. He had achieved many great successes in the wars and he had supported the king Sargon when he handled the throne. He had a strong, powerful and athletic body despite being around forties. He was handsome and gentleman. He was good at using his sword and keeping his promises. He was ordered especially to protect the king's daughter Enheduanna and the city Ur. He was raised as a major when he came to Ur. He was a clever and experienced strategist. He was commanding the quarters and the soldiers and doing the best things to provide the security. Despite all these talents, his weaknesses were women and alcohol. For him, there was no difference between a beautiful woman and a pitch of wine. He was ready to be drunk with any of these. What if there were a beautiful woman with a pitcher of wine? Then the matters started. His military courage that he earned against his enemies was his characteristic feature of him for women in his social life. Without keeping his words, directly expressing his ideas to face his target could be a nonsense behaviour according to some people and events but it was an ordinary behaviour for the commander Namtar. He was not only brave but also unashamed. He had blurted out many things daring to be refused. He had a night affair almost with all the nuns in the temple. Everybody was in the opinion that the military uniform suited him well.

Nakurtum followed Namtar and they came to the room. They both bent in respect and greeted her. Nakurtum wanted to speak:

"Holy Sister, if I would be no use here, I want to return to my work.'"

"No, my dear nun, I want especially you to be here, too. Please, come and sit beside me. Commander

Namtar, please, you sit here, too." she said pointing to the sofa on her right next to the wall. She went on speaking while the commander sat where he was showed:

"Dear Namtar who was one of the greater commanders of my father and the guard of me and the city. I called you due to an important duty."

"I see, the High Priestess otherwise you would meet me with a box full of beers and dancers. I also have news for you." he said smiling teasingly.

The commander never missing any entertainments like the ordinary Ur people, He never kept himself from accompanying Enheduanna in any entertainments to protect the city because everything he needed at those nights were available in the temple such as sex, woman, drinks and worship. For him, these nights were used to meet a needing rather than worshipping. Enheduanna responded smiling slightly and teasingly:

"Don't worry, you are my guest in the evening, too. I may have different surprises than the usual. Firstly, you speak, I am looking forward to hearing your news."

"I have no doubt, my princess. The troops that we had sent to the wild people in the desert are doing their jobs well. They are disabling every tribe one by one. they will returned in a great victory soon." said he and leaned back on the wall. He dried his sweat running down from his forehead using the back of his left hand.

"Perfect, those barbarians had needed such a lesson for a long time. They never intend to be modern. They have only their swords. You know that I have a duty here as a High Priest for four years, I have tried to make this temple and the others operate as well as before and make them worthy for public and Gods. I completed the missing parts. I did what hadn't been done before. I worked day and night without stopping. All the temples in our country make effort for the happiness of our Gods and the peace of our public but I have made a decision. I will start applying this decision from tomorrow on. There may be the ones who won't be pleased with my decision and will try to provoke the public against me. You will intervene here."

"You know that your father, the king Sargon had sent me here to protect the city and you. I am always with you. No doubt that I would do my best to do my job. What is your decision, you the Holy Sister, may I learn it?"

"I will make this temple solely for the Goddess Inanna-the only owner of the earth and the sky, shining like a full moon at night and the God of love and war. I will remove the other Gods from Ur. Only Inanna would be adorn in Ur."

Namtar startled against what he had heard. His shock was visible on his face. He changed his position on the sofa he was sitting crossed legs. He pulled one of his feet back and sat on the other foot.

"Are you aware how dangerous this decision is, you the Holy Sister?" His words were interrupted by Enheduanna. She was expecting his full obedience for her thoughts and plans. She responded in a slight angry and stern tone:

"Commander, why do you think I have called you here? Your duty is this. You have to obey me fully if I am the High Priest of this land, the daughter of the king Sargon and Princess Enheduanna."

"You have misunderstood me, the Holy Sister. I am always at your service. Of course,I will obey your orders but I can't make my soldiers carry the things. This is very risky because they and the public adorn the same Gods that you would take out of the temples in deed. This may cause annoyance among the soldiers."

"Yes commander, we have thought and planned what to be done. After the entertainments have finished, the temple has been emptied and cleaned, I would want the servicers to carry the statues of Gods and the altars which were wrapped in clothes and resemble something else one by one. My scribes are preparing the salvation documents of all the slaves with my assistant Amare. After all the Gods and altars were loaded in the vehicle, you and your soldiers would take statues and the free slaves out of the city. You would take the vehicles somewhere deserted out of the city and make them buried in the land. Then, you would help the slaves get in a ship and leave them somewhere having a boundary to a gulf but not to our country.You have to do all of these in only one day. I may need you in the city later."

Don't worry, my Holy Sister, I would leave half of my troop here, at your service."

"That's great, the commander! Everything is clear, I

think. You will be my guest in the evening so you could ask me whatever you want without hesitation. We still have time."

"Thank you, my Holy Sister. Let me arrange a ship to carry the slaves. If I do it in the evening, I could miss the entertainment." he said smiling teasingly again.

"Of course, the commander, you may leave. I trust you, let's see you in the evening."

The commander stood up. He returned when he was about to leave the room bending in respect. He spoke in a doubtful and implying tone:

"My princess, it has been reported that the two soldiers getting in the ship with you last evening haven't returned to the quarter yet. The lieutenant Eluti said that they hadn't gotten in the boat. Do you have any information about this?" he asked.

Enheduanna realising where the commander getting the conversation at spoke short:

"Yes, the lieutenant is right, the soldiers coming with me have returned to the quarter. I think two of them seemed escaped. You must be more careful commander, You must protect your soldiers."

"You may be right, my princess, see you in the evening."

Nakurtum had listened to the whole conversation silently and carefully. Enheduanna was carrying out the planned they made yesterday exactly but the behaviours of the commander had worried her.

"What a smarty man he is." said she.

Enheduanna smiled. She pinched her face. She responded self assuredly and kiddingly:

"Don't worry, my priest, I know the Commander Namtar very well. He has been coming after me to possess me for years. He knows that he has to carry out my orders to be able to achieve this aim."

"You know the best, my lady. The offer serving ceremonies have been over, preparations for feasting have been started. Let me check around."

"Ok, you beautiful priest Everything is how we set yesterday, no change. Inform me when anything important happens. Send me the Priest Akiya who is responsible for the priests."

"Your orders, my Holy Sister." she said leaving the room.

She passed through the corridors quickly in short steps as usual. One of the most important characteristics of Nakurtum that she always looked down when she walked. She was the last person to realise if the colors of the walls were changed. She went to the kitchen first. She looked into the large pots placed on the wooden fires. She checked the beer pitchers set on the table in the corner of the kitchen. She examined the sand dishes full of fruit placed on the shelves on which the high and tall cabinet leaning on the other wall stood. The damp in the kitchen was so thick as to sweat the people in seconds. There was a heavy odour and it was hard to breathe here. She turned to head cook:

"Is everything ready?" she asked to the Priest Utu.

Priest Utu was an old man in his sixties who had spent all his life in the temple and served it a great deal. His mother was one of the priestesses in the temple and was working as a cook. She had born her child after she was pregnant due to the seclusion. Since then, he had been a servant in the kitchen.

He was a sweet and short man with his white hair and beards, large stomach due to tasting the meal and drinking beer too much. He responded to Priest Nakurtum in his thick, mature, so tired, shaking and excited tone:

"Everything is ready, the priestess, The remaining food in the altar are being gathered now. The tables in the hall in which the entertainment be performed would be set after they have been brought."

Nakurtum asked in a stern tone once more:

"You have sent the remaining ones for dry, haven't you or waited for me to order you?"

The head cook Utu responded in a shy tone:

"Not at all, priestess, everything has been done how it must be. He thought in his heart: You dirty bitch, I shouldn't ask you of course."

the meat, fruit and vegetables more than necessary were sliced, ropes were strung to in the reserved places in the temple and kept for dry. then, they were put in the sacks and placed in the depots.

Nakurtum passed to the hall in which the altars were situated. There was an altar in front of every God statuette belong to that God. She checked all the altars one by one. It was clear that all the food had been gathered but the altars hadn't been cleaned yet. She checked the hands and feet of the Gods. They didn't seem cleaned. She got angry:

"Priestess Aşaru, Priestess Aşaru!" she screamed loud. The sounds of running sandals had been heard. Little later, priestess Aşaru appeared in front of her. The priestess Aşaru was a slant-eyed, short and a fat woman. It felt as it her small nose was lost between her fat cheeks. Her thin eyebrows were like the traces on her eyes. She was a hard-working and a meticulous woman. She would immediately be excited or shaken when something was incomplete or wrong. Nakurtum showed her anger asking:

"What a shame, what a carelessness is this, priestess Aşaru?"

68   Priestess Aşaru was one of the most experienced priestess spending her whole life in this temple. She had never married and she had never entered even the seclusion room. There were rumors in the temple that she had been still virgin. She was rumored that she kept herself for the God Enki. She couldn't have the chance to rise as she couldn't learn how to read/write and was raised to the highest level that she could be which was the altar responsibility. Priestess Aşaru responded in an embarrassed tone:

"My Holy Sister, two of the nuns working under my order haven't been around today. I searched for them but couldn't find. They may be prostituting somewhere else. I and my two assistants are working now. We started to clean one by one. We have been able to clean only those so far. We will finish till the supper, I promise you."

"Find priestess Nintu at once and tell her that I have ordered. . Get three nuns out of there and clean everywhere before the sun set. If I saw even a trace of blood, you will find yourself prostituting in the taverns, Priestess Aşaru!" she said turning her head and passed the largest garden of the temple where the entertainment would be held.

The priests were organizing all the tables near each other. The priestesses were placing the chairs. The various flowers picked up from the garden were waiting in the cars to be set at the tables. Nakurtum inhaled the perfect, freshing odour of the purple hyacinths feeling that sense that the spring has come. Near them, there were the bunches of pure white magnolia flowers shedding green on the earth, breezing at long nights. A large platform was being prepared in front of the entrance for musicians and dancers. During the entertainment, lyres, flutes, tambourines, timbals and arps were ready to take their places to help the guests experience a perfect music experience. The musicians have completed their preparations and worn their elegant, sexually attractive, half transparent or rope made clothes. The one meter height and five meters wide wooden platform on which Enheduanna and her assistants would sit, the carpet made of the best ropes in different decorations and colours was brought down, her tablet had been prepared and was waiting to be decorated.

Before Enheduanna, in the temple, offers were made, entertainments were organized and the nuns devoting their bodies to the Gods were staying in seclusion rooms everyday. Enheduanna seeing that things couldn't be carried out completely or insufficiently and many things were wasted in these busy days had set the offering day a day before the resting day of everyone which means just a day in a week so, those who want to make offer on the day did it, had his supper in the temple, had fun drinking and eating till late hours at night, went to his/her house and got rest throughout the day. No one had complained about this change but the widows, homeless and poor people, children who could be badly effected by this change were provided food every evening in the temple.

After Nakurtum checked the large garden, she came down to the seclusion room situated on the base floor of the temple. There were twenty rooms here which were separated by walls. All the rooms were carefully designed for all kinds of needs. The rooms were illuminated by the small windows so large as heads on the day. There were oil candles for the nights. The ground was covered by colorful and decorated carpets.

The wooden, large, double beds covered by soft clothes and pillars washed in perfumed water had been placed just opposite the entrance doors. On the right of the entrance, there were hangers made of reeds for the persons who would go seclusion to hang their clothes and sofas made of reeds. There was a small table in front of the sofa and a small mirror on its wall. The pitcher on the table was sometimes full of beer, sometimes wine or sometimes water. It completely depended on the visitor's desire. There was a small lyre to be played in every room. It was waiting for the musical ceremony for the guests while they were sipping their best drinks at the beginning of the hot night spent for Inanna. All the rooms surrounded a yard in the middle. There were sofa on which the women to enter the seclusion room could sit and wait. The sofas surrounded the small pool in the middle. The firebrands situated on the ground on four metal legs were to illuminate the yard. The man wanting to have sexuality came here, had his name registered by the responsible nun and said: "Calling the Goddess Inanna on your behalf" throwing a silver coin to one of the waiting nuns in the yard or selecting one of the women presented herself as an offer. He would take that woman/nun and went to one of the room. It was a kind of marriage agreement in deed. It was formalizing a one time coupling in the presence of the God.

The charge taken by the Holy Sister belonged to the temple. They believed that Inanna had resurrected in their own body due to this relation and felt happy due to the satisfaction they had during the sex. The pregnant women bore in the temple, brought their children up here. When the children grew up, they either used to work and live in the temple or among the public. Enheduanna's father was a nun's child. He grew up in the temple, worked at high levels in the palace and became the king in the end. These nuns were accepted as holy by the public. They were respected a great deal, too. The Holy Sisters had to wear a headscarf to be distinguished from other women. During the times they didn't serve the men, they used to do the ordinary work like all the other nuns.

When Nakurtum saw that everything in place and organized in the seclusion room, she felt relieved. Expressing a well-done to the responsible Nun Urnina, she headed towards the room of the priest Akiya who was responsible for all the Priests. Akiya had been a soldier in deed, he had served in the military for years and joined many wars but he had lost his genital organ with a sword attack in a war. For this reason, he had devoted his body and existence to the Gods like the other priests resembling him. They were trying to do all kinds of work in the temple and also serving in the seclusion room for the men who wanted to have homosexual relation. As they didn't have organs, There was no problem if they were with the priestesses or work with them. The priest Akiya was tall, giant and a short haired. man. He had a large, shapeless nose in the middle of his beardless face. He was responsible for the priests as he was raised to be lieutenant due to his successes and education in his military service. He was a rude and unsympathetic man at the end of his fifties.

When Nakurtum entered the room, Priest Akiya stood leaving the tablet on the ground he had been reading.

"Welcome, the priestess, What in the world, you have come here?"

Nakurtum crossed her arms under her chests. She stretched her right foot forward, leaned her hips on the right and looked into his eyes surrendered by his wrinkled face under his whitened eyebrows.

"Have you left any open place in the temple, Priest Akiya?"

Akiya couldn't understand what she meant. He had already difficulty in understand what this priestess meant. Whenever she came, either she caused a problem or something unexpected occurred. Even if nothing happened, she would do something to make him unhappy.

"What do you mean, the priestess?"

Nakurtum said smiling:

"You are talking about the wind, I asked for that."

The priest Akiya understanding the remark smiled.

"My priestess is as usual beautiful and sympathetic."

Nakurtum, feeling appreciated due to this sentence raised her chests inhaling a deep breath. She continued talking teasingly:

"You are so calm as usual, priest Akiya. The High Priestess is calling you to her room. I have come to inform you."

"Her orders, I will attend immediately. Is there a problem, do you have any information?" he asked scratching his hair using his left hand.

"Of course, there is the priest Akiya. The problem is very big. There is a very large army waiting in front of the walls of the temple. They say that they certainly want a Holy Priest for seclusion this evening. We couldn't know what to do."

Nakurtum started giggling in her heart but didn't reflect it. The priest Akiya had frightened and worried at the same time.

"I may have lost my genital organ in the war but my proud to be a man is still how it must be from the birth." he murmured and continued in a shaking and frightened tone:

"But my lady, how it could be? Please free me from such things, I have never been volunteer for things like that." he could say.

Nakurtum sent out a loud laughter.

"Goddesses make you happy, priest Akiya. I am just kidding. I think I know what the matter is. The High Sister is thinking to sacrifice you as an offer tomorrow but pretend not to know about it."

Nakurtum giggled in her heart again and left the room. Akiya started shaking again. He felt a sudden awe. In a low tone of voice, he spoke after she had gone:

74   How can you do such a thing to a man of sixties? What is my guilt? Why do they choose me instead of many snob priests?" he said.

He started smoothing and cleaning his clothes and hair. He headed towards the floor of the Holy Sister.

Nakurtum checking the whole temple ended up in the scribe room which she used with Amare and on which the same floor having the room Enheduanna did her usual tasks in. She was soaked up by the sweat and her clothes were stuck to her body. All the beauty of her body and curving firm physic were visible under the cloth covering her body. She lay on the sofa at once. She was very tired and thirsty. She turned Amare and asked:

"How about the salvation documents, have you finished preparing them?"

"We finished in the end but I felt very tired. I would take them to the High Priest for sealing. How about you? Have you finished your work?"

"Yes, I have finished but I am beaten. It is very hard to carry out the things when you aren't with me. I don't have enough energy to join the celebrations in the evening.

Amare stood up, she smoothed her clothes and stretched her hand out to Nakurtum:

"Come on, stand up, the sun is about to set, let's take the documents to the Holy Sister and then go to the bath. We feel relaxed after bathing." she said.

Nakurtum stood up holding Amare's hand. They walked to the top story towards Enheduanna's room.

While ascending the stairs, they met the Priest Aki-ya descending with a blushed face and murmuring himself. When he saw Nakurtum, he continued saying: "shame on you, dear nun, shame on you!" and descended near the nuns.

Nakurtum laughed loud. She said turning towards the priest Akiya:

"I love you, priest Akiya, I am glad you are with us." and continued laughing.

Amare not understanding what was going on poked Nakurtum curiously and asked:

"Have I missed anything?"

"Nothing, my usual jokes on him, dear nun. I wanted to have fun with him but I think I have made him really angry this time. "

She told her what had happened till they arrived at Enheduanna's room. They came to the door laughing. When they came in the room after knocking, Enheduanna was busy with writing something with her reed pencil on her hair tablet. When she realised that they had come, she invited both of them to sit. Amare was the first to speak:

"My princess, we have prepared the salvation documents of the slaves under your order. Only your sealing remained."

Enheduanna got the seal and handed out to Amare looking at her face.

"Please, seal the documents on my behalf. I am a bit busy. I will go out and make observations. I need to make some calculations for this. Let's go out together and I will teach you how to do it."

The nuns felt utmost joy. This was a great opportunity because these things couldn't be taught everybody. They were the observation works done only by the High Priests or Holy Sisters.

Nakurtum stretched the tablets one by one and Amare performed the cylinder sealed on the tablets. They finished the work quickly. They started looking forward to going up to the room on the top of the temple in which the observations were made. During the waiting, they watched Enheduanna's calculations with her soft, perfect, white, long and thin fingers on the tablet. She was sitting crossed legs, her head bent down, her beautiful hair dropped down her forehead. The odour of her perfume made of the seeds of various flowers that she wore everyday before wearing her clothes, combined with her skin's odour gave the room a perfect feeling. The room was feeling love and Enheduanna. When she finished her calculations, she asked the nuns:

"Everything was as we had spoken, weren't they, my dear girls. I hope there is nothing wrong."

Amare jumped into while Nakurtum was about to speak:

"There is nothing wrong, the Holy Sister. Everything has been prepared how you wanted. The only thing we would do is to take out blankets and clothes from the temple depot and wrap the statues after the ceremonies."

Enheduanna nodding her head:

"Very well, dear daughters, I trust in you. We will success this all together. I will have a surprise for you after we have succeeded." she said smiling.

The nuns felt more joyful. They had realised how honorable and chance to be with a Holy Sister like Enheduanna once more. Before Enheduanna came, the temple was ruled by an old, thoughtless, stern and intolerable Holy Priest. He walked all around all day with the stick in his hand to give orders and reprehend the people. Nakurtum thought almost all the time if they were serving the Gods or this old looney man. Both Nakurtum and Amare were no different than the ordinary servants working all day. After Enheduanna came, they had been themselves again. The efforts they had been making to the temple since they were a child had been rewarded by Enheduanna. They had been the two, most important rulers out of three of the temple and Ur due to her. they had gained power and post not only for themselves but also they had earned honor for their families. They owed her not only their posts, private rooms, separate dinner tables, the smartest clothes, the best perfumes, the necklaces and rings made of precious stones such as emerald and agate; but also everything.

Enheduanna and the two nuns went up to the room on the top floor which was prohibited to everyone except the Holy Sister and the priest responsible for the observation work. This room situated on the four columns, whose surrounding was open and had a ceiling was on the top of the temple and Enheduanna's personal room at the same time. Amare and Nakurtum looked around in surprise because there were a lot of wooden embossed or metal tools that they couldn't understand around the room.

When the nuns looked down, they understood that the temple was very high. They felt dizzy due to the height and they felt necessary to hold the edges. It was breezing slightly, caressing their faces and carrying their odours to the calm deserts behind them. All of their fears swept away by the breeze when they saw the perfect city Ur lying below them from the highest point above. The city Ur dazed their eyes as it was surrendered by farms and gardens like colorful carpets; its sea told by the traders, reaching the far seas and combined with Buranun sea like a long line; the lights tearing through the darkness of the evening like stars penetrating the nights.

the astronomic observations were vital for the Sumerians because a society whose economy based on agriculture must know when to cultivate the crops, to reap the productions, when the water of the river would rise or fall. For this reason, they were making astronomic observations and noting the information they had gained on the tablets.

For Enheduanna, astronomic observations had another purpose. It was to learn when Dumuzi would be salvaged from the underground he was captivated in and marry Inanna, otherwise it was impossible for her to know the time of seeding the land and re-surfacing of lives which means the start of the spring. Detecting the time properly, she must perform the holy marriage ritual and organize celebrations for the fertilizing lands with the surfacing of Dumuzi again. Everything must be done on time and correctly to make Inanna happy.

Enheduanna showing the reeds through the sub ceiling and just over them in a shape of crescent to the nuns said:

"My nuns, the reed you have seen shows the path of the sun from its rising to its setting. The sun is rising from the point which the reed shows with its front and sets down from the point which the reed shows with the end point just behind us. This line could change everyday so it must be checked daily. The priest Alulim are doing this on my behalf."

Amare and Nakurtum were listening to Enheduanna and repeating her words by their hearts to memorize. Nakurtum had a question in her mind about them:

"Then, my Holy Sister, If this line you told us follows changes everyday, how does this change happen?"

Enheduanna liked the question very much.

"Very well Nakurtum, very good question. It was like this today. It will slightly bend towards the south tomorrow. You know that the sun goes through a thicker line in the summer and a thinner in the winter. In winter, it stays at the top line in a shorter time than in summer but this bending is very small, it is very hard to see it daily. We generally detect this change monthly." she said and turned to the nuns with her reed pencil and her tablet:

Look, there are many stars in the sky now. I will mark here eight of them. Then you will look up and tell me the places of these stars.

And she put eight marks on the tablet with her pencil. Then she handed out to the nuns for them to see. After Nakurtum and Amare examined these marks carefully, they started to find the stars ordered in the same style in the sky. It didn't take long. Nakurtum stretched out her hand saying:

"I have found, it is right up there. and showed the place of the star cluster with her thumb."

Amare realised it after she had showed it. Enheduanna was pleased as the nuns had learned this so quickly.

"Very good for you, you will succeed this work. I know that the name of the star cluster you have found is the taurus of the sky. It is called taurus because when the stars are combined, an ox like shape emerges. There are eleven more from these star cluster. We call them zodiacs. I will teach them to you later. Now, pay attention to the path which the sun follows above our heads. Does it conflict with the star cluster that you have found?"

The nuns stood under the bow shaped reed and checked if it is in the same line with the star cluster. They said all together:

"No, my lady, It is not exactly over it but there is a slight difference."

"Very well, my dear nuns. I will measure that difference and calculate how many days later the ox star cluster will conflict with the line that the sun follows. Watch how I measure it and I will tell you later how to do it. The best time to measure this is during the sun rise. When the sun rises in ox zodiac, it means that the spring has come.

She got two reeds, one end of whose could be stabled and curved. She made a few things with them. She noted on the tablet. Then she calculated. She turned to the nuns and said:

"There are still four days to the one that we wait for."

Amare couldn't help asking:

"My holy Sister, are there four days to the Holy Marriage Celebrations?"

Enheduanna nodding her head said:

"Yes, Amare, there are four days to the re-surfacing of Dumuzi and the Holy Marriage Ceremonies. We will see the crescent a day before and the next morning will be the day we have been looking forward to."

"But this is great! It is possible for you to see the future from now."

Enheduanna sent out a short laughter.

"Yes, my beautiful nun, it may be to see the future."

Amare asked again in a surprise:

"But my lady, in the temple schools, we had been taught that only the Gods could know the future. How could it happen? I couldn't understand."

Enheduanna held Amare's neck using her right hand, pulled towards her and leaned on her chest.

"Do you think the Gods know about their futures? I am sure that Enlil doesn't know where Enki is. The fortune is not what you are given but what you get by yourself. The future is in the hand of everybody. If you cultivate barley, you crop barley, you can't expect to crop wheat. Everybody's future is based on their decisions, don't forget it. If you let yourself down here, you die. If you don't let, you will continue living. You can't get back the arrow to its bow. The only thing that you can't change about your future is the time. Look, the shining star here is the evening star. It is the brilliant face of Inanna. One of the eleven moving stars. We call them as moving stars because they don't stay stable like the other stars. They are always moving. Come on, let's make our preparations, go to the ceremony area. and take our places. The rising noise shows that the feast and the entertainment have already started.

The two young nuns felt surprised by Enheduanna's last words They were opposite of what they had been taught by that time and this would neither be first or the last. The Holy Sister continued surprising them. They went to the room of the Holy Sister. they helped her wear the special costume for the ceremony. The ceremony dress was donated with gold pieces, stretching down to her ankles, having slashes on both sides, making her chests slightly visible. They made her hair and put down her scarf. They placed the cap having golden leaves on it. They helped her wear the crown made of flowers, symbolizing Inanna-the abundance and reproduction. They helped her wear the wristlets made of the same flowers on each wrist of her. They sprayed the best perfumes to her ear backs and wrists. They put the rings and ornaments made of precious stones.

Lastly, they smoothing their scarfs and clothes, combining their hands in front of them passed to the ceremony hall which is the larges garden of the temple following Enheduanna.

When they came to the big garden, they saw that all the Ur people sat at the tables and when the tables were full, the remainings crouched down and started eating with their wives and children. They went to the wooden platform reserved for them. They sat all together-Enheduanna between them, Amare and Nakurtum were on the sides. The servants seeing that they had come started to set their tables at once. Boiled lamb, fried carps, bulgur pilaf, soup made of flour and milk, leek with bean, lettuce salad, boiled duck, bread dessert and chicken pasty had been donated their tables with. (20) They started eating with a big appetite. They were both eating their feast and watching the people in the garden. The garden was like a festival area. It looked a large field due to the flowers placed on the tables. The wind was carrying perfect odours. Something caught Amare's attention in a moment. All the nuns and slaves were working in the garden but there were no priests working. She pulled herself back slightly and spoke to Nakurtum behind Enheduanna:

"Hey, hey, priestess Nakurtum!"

Her worry and curiosity can be deduced from her voice tone being so soft as not to disturb Enheduanna. Nakurtum hearing Amare got on her:

"What again, let us eat our feast as we please!"

The tiredness and the hunger that her body had due to working all day limited her movements and speaking. She went on eating and watching without caring her. Amare didn't stop and spoke again. Nakurtum could bear no more and asked when she felt sure that she would continue speaking if she didn't respond:

"What, what happened?"

"The priests!"

"What is wrong with the priests?"

"The priests, they aren't here." Nakurtum started looking all around her more carefully. She was right, there was no priest, even one of them. There was something wrong with this. She responded to Amare:

"Yes, you are right, none of them are here."

They went on eating their feast turning their eyes on their tables. They were both examining their surroundings curiously and eating. Meanwhile, they were feeling very nervous about the non existence of the priests. As they have realised it, Enheduanna had certainly realised or she didn't?

Enheduanna could guess what they were speaking of even if she couldn't hear them. She spoke in her heart in a soft smile:

"You are about to learn it, dear girls."

After a time, eating has finished. The nuns, female servants and slaves started gathering up the dishes, spoons and other remainings things from the tables. They left the bread on the tables because the beers would be delivered in the cups and breads would be a snack.

Musician Nuns started taking their places reserved for them in the front area of the garden with their lyres, flutes, drums and harps. Behind the entrance of the temple, the dance girls were trying to smooth their clothes and their hair. The atmosphere in the garden was great. The public started to drink their beers via the reeds out of the cups and was looking forward to seeing the dance and hearing the music. A few young people in the public whistled to invite them to start the ceremony in a shorter time. No matter how much they tried, Musicians, dancer nuns were waiting for Enheduanna's sign. Enheduanna hadn't given that sign despite all the things being already ready.

After a short time, something unexpected and interesting happened. Instead of dancers, priests came in a line through the entrance of the temple and walked near the garden wall passing by Enheduanna. After a time, a loud laughter broke up among the public. They were watching the pass ceremony of the priests laughing lying on the ground. All the nuns including Nakurtum and Amare joined the laughter ceremony.

The top of the head of the priests was bald and the mid section of their heads was specially shaved but the round was untouched. The public seeing the priests in such a case for the first time felt the utmost joy. It was impossible to say the same for the priests, of course. When the pass ceremony of the priests had ended and they returned to the temple, Enheduanna stood up. She got the lyre made of seven string and the combination of perfect silver and wood. There was an ox figure with golden horns curving from bottom to top. She accorded her lyre hitting the strings a few times. Then she started singing one of her best chants. The lyres of the musician nuns were accompanying her. The crowd was fixed on Enheduanna. Her poem with her soft voice scattering the silence in the temple garden, echoing through the walls had become the song of the night and came out softly out of her lips:

The Holy Queen of the sky, Inanna,
Greetings for you,
She is the only Holy,
Greetings for you,
The Holy Queen of the sky, Inanna,
Greetings for you,
The pure firebrand illuminating the sky,
The Holy light shining like a sun,
The Holy Queen of the sky, Inanna,
Greetings for you,

The brilliant queen of the Holy Anunnaki,
Holy in the sky and on the earth,
Beautified with great horns
The oldest son of Suen, Inanna,
Greetings for you,
The greatness and respect of her magnificence
About her utmost dignity
And in her sky when the evening comes
About her brilliantly appearing
Like a pure firebrand in the sky
About her fire setting illumination
From south to north,
Acknowledged across all the lands
About the holiness of the owner of the sky
let's make a song!

Enheduanna finished her poem and let the entertainment start which was expected by everybody in
a great excitement.

The people had already been captured by the joy
and entertainment in the garden. Meanwhile, Amare
could no longer help asking that question in her heart.

"My beautiful lady of all beauties and the Holy Sister of Inanna, Why are these priests in this case? Why
have they shaved the top of their heads?" Enheduanna leaned her softly and said:

"Their heads are shaved just as you wear scarf.
They will walk around in the temple and the city in
that style."

The temple priestesses had to walk around in the
temple and the city wearing their scarves otherwise

they were punished severely. Enheduanna had realised how difficult it is to distinguish between the nuns working in the temple from the normal people on the offer day. She had ordered the priests to shave the top of their heads to be distinguished from other men. From that on, this tradition continued the same.

While the public was enjoying themselves and drinking, the dancers were performing their best dance via the rhythms with their curving bodies and distorting the men of Ur. The men and women apparently getting lost due to the effect of beer and apple wine started dancing with the dancers. They were getting rid of the tiredness of the week shouting, screaming and enjoying crazily. Later at night, the dancers started taking off the transparent costumes and danced showing all her talents in dance and their bodies. Whenever they curved their bellies, their hips and chests like the fruit ready to be picked up were shaking in accordance with the rhythm of dance and music. At those times when the players started to play their fastest songs, the Ur women, unable to sit still started to take off their clothes and started to accompany the dancer nuns. The men were distorted by these attractive and dazing dances rather than beer and wine. They were cheering them up clapping, screaming and whistling.

While the entertainment continued, Amare and Nakurtum left Enheduanna there to do their usual works. Nakurtum getting down to the basement where the seclusion rooms were situated went to have information about the nuns and the public women who would seclude with Urnina. Whomever wanted to seclude couldn't enter those rooms. The nuns and the women out of the temple wishing to seclude had to have

Urnina write register their names before. Not only the women who wanted to pray devoting themselves to Inanna had to seclude themselves but also the young girls who wanted to marry. Required by the rules, the young, virgin girls who wanted to marry could do it only with the document Urnina prepared after they had coupled with a foreign man, sacrifice their virginity in the name of Inanna and donate the charge they got for Inanna. Most of those girls were brought by their families for seclusion. The girls who wanted to marry but not allowed by their parents had the right to seclude with the permission of the Holy Sister. Urnina was one of the children who were born in the temple and his mother was a priestess.

After Enheduanna came, she realised that Urnina was one of the nuns having always seclusion so she had made her responsible for seclusion rooms. Her being tall, long haired, having big breasts and her thin belly were enough to make her one of the most attractive nuns of the temple. None of her seclusions were empty. There were a lot of men competing to be with her. She had also many fans who wanted to donate all their property to the temple not only a few silver coins.

She was in deed a temple whore like all the other nuns. In addition to being one of the most beautiful nuns of the temple, she was a very clever woman. She had graduated from the temple school with the appreciations of all her teachers and she started to be a nun working as an assistant of healer which was one of the best jobs. The subject she was the best at and felt interested in was herbals. She dealt with this till she became the responsible seclusion. She owed her calm personality to the herbal mixtures she had prepared by herself.

Nakurtum checked all the rooms and the yard one by one and asked Urnina:

"How many persons have their names registered?"

Urnina looked at the tablet she took out of her pocket:

"Including me, there are twenty-two persons, priestess Nakurtum. Fourteen temple nuns and eight public people." she said.

"How many of them are the virgins coming for marriage?"

"There are only three girls for it."

"Don't let them get in the seclusion room, tell them that they will be secluded in the Holy Marriage ceremony held four days later."

"Your orders, Priestess Nakurtum." she said inserting the tablet back into her pocket and went to her room to exclude the names of the virgins from the list.

Nakurtum, finishing her work in the seclusion rooms returned to Enheduanna again. After nodding to say that everything was ok, she continued having her entertainment.

Amare was in the small depots built in an order along the garden walls in the temple. The cereals were placed in different depots according to their types and the dried fruits, vegetables and meat were stored in different depots as well. Whatever cultivated, cropped, hunted in Ur for the temple were stored in these depots. All these products were for the temple but the whole public could share these products. This was a precaution against infertility but it was also the other way for the people to share equally whatever belonged to Ur. When the cropping was less or insufficient, they were also sent to the other countries. Depots were one of the most protected places of the city. They were consciously built in the small garden in the temple. The garden door being locked all the time was the opposite of the main entrance door of the temple. It was easy to be observed by the soldiers on duty.

The responsible priests were carrying the products such as cereals, flour, fruits and vegetables to be delivered to the public after the ceremony. Amare looked for the priest Endugagga who was responsible for the depots but couldn't find him. He was an old soldier, too. As he worked in weapon and supply depots in his military service, he was given the same duty in the temple. He would keep the stock data in the small room at the end of the depots. He was an honest man but he was rumored to drink stealing beer or wine bottles among the priests. Despite the rumor, no one had seen him doing it. It was clear that he was keen on drinking which made the priests think so.

The lands cultivated-cropped and the animals fed by the Sumer public belonged to the temple. They used to get their share from the crops and the works. Those who prefer to work in the fields and other types of works could get their charges too. As all the crops, including the meat of the animals which were sacrificed belong to the God, they were stored in the depots of the temple. This included everything such as the clothes woven by tailors, the carpets woven by the villager woman and the chairs made by the carpenter.

On some certain days of the week, They were shared to the people equally registering them in lists after the ceremonies. The people used to get their shares and went to their homes. They used to meet their supplies in such a way throughout the week.

Amare asked the first priest she met where Endugagga was. When the priest said that she was in her room a while ago but he didn't know where she is now, her face changed. She clenched her teeth and fisted her hands.

"Fetch her at once!" she screamed. The frightened priest jumped in fear and disappeared.

Amare, leaving the depots and coming to the tables where the delivery would be made, checked the each sack piled up in an order. She learned from the registry man for how many people these sacks were prepared. She warned them to do their best and not make any mistakes.

Then she came to the barracks in which the slaves were living situated in the smallest garden of the rear temple. The slaves having fun drinking by themselves on the tables that they placed in front of the barracks stood up and greeted her. Amare, getting the three slaves, wanted them to get ten blankets from the depot and necessary amount of rope, then entered the deserted temple due to the entertainment through the side door. She got one of the firebrands hung near the entrance door. She came to the altar hall and started to light the firebrands one by one. After each light, the inside was getting more illuminated and the places where the light fell was becoming more visible. She could feel the strangeness in the room only when she lit the third firebrand. She couldn't believe in her eyes or didn't want to believe. Before lighting the fourth one, she stretched it forward and started to pace in the hall. She saw that the finger tips of the God statuettes had been broken, cut off and shattered in a horror. She lit all the other firebrands in the hall and the whole disaster appeared. Her jaw dropped. She looked around herself without knowing what to do. Her knees loosened. She crouched down when her hands and feet started trembling. She combined her hands on her head. She could only say: "Oh my God, what the hell is this?"

The entertainment was going on in the big garden. The singers and some players had left the stage. Only the melodies played by the lyres of the two nuns had been echoing which meant that the night was about to be over. The public was sitting at their tables and sipping the last drops of their drinks. Some started to move slowly towards the area where the supplies were delivered still bearing the enjoyment. Some were whistling, some were murmuring the last song he/she could remember and some were trying to walk slightly shaking due to the effect of the alcohol.

The Holy Sister Enheduanna, one side of whom the commander Namtar and the other side of whom Nakurtum were sitting was sitting at her table and watching the entertainment and the public drinking their cold beers. They were joyful. Enheduanna pretending to be laughing at the bad jokes of the commander gently was trying to handle the matter and finish the night. The commander feeling more drank after every glass was blurting his hidden love for Enheduanna in his stammering words. This was making enheduanna and Nakurtum very joyful.

Amare silently whispered to Enheduanna's ear from Nakurtum's side.

"The Holy Sister, There is a problem where the altars were situated. One person or people had broken the statues except for Inanna.

Enheduanna feeling surprised what she heard fingered her hair backward, and adjusted her scarf. She turned to Amare and said:

"We can deal with it after the entertainment." and sipped her glass on the table a few times.

Enheduanna gestured Nakurdum to move her chair forward and Amare to sit between them. She put a glass in front of Amare filling it with cold beer.

"Someone must have done it on our behalf, but who?"

Amare's worry and horror had reflected her voice tone.

"The priest Endugagga is not where he must be, he is lost, my lady." she said.

Nakurtum hearing what was spoken, responded saying:

"He must certainly asleep somewhere after drinking too much alcohol." Enheduanna looked at the two nuns smiling:

"Don't think of it now my dear daughters, everything is ok, continue enjoying yourself. We will look into it later."

She got her lyre and started playing one of her favorite song. The commander affected by the song stood up and started dancing out of control. He turned around raising his hands and sometimes stepping hard on the ground in accordance with the rhythm.

Meanwhile, Nakurtum stretched out Amare's package wrapped in a piece of cloth.

"This had been sent to you while you were checking the things. It was given to one of the priestesses to be delivered to you."

Amare felt curious and started releasing the cloth tied with a rope. A small hair tablet appeared in it. She put it into her pocket after reading and went on drinking her beer getting her glass. She pretended not to hear Nakurtum's questions such as: "Who had sent it?, what was its contents?" ETC.

Enheduanna turning to the commander feeling tired after the music and dance asked:

"Commander Namtar, what do you think about my decision to make the temple solely for Inanna? You haven't spoken about this yet."

Namtar, sipping a large amount of wine from his glass set it on the table. He responded after drying his mouth with the back of his left hand.

"My princess, nothing will change for me, be sure."

"What do you mean, commander?"

"All the Gods are the same to me. If the Gods are living in these temples built for them, how can they be kept in an altar hall despite their being almighty and able to do everything? I can't understand it!" he said sending out a loud laughter and finished his wine glass grabbing on the table in one sip. then he left it in front of Enheduanna and said:

"If my princess honors me, I can drink one more glass for her beauty."

When Enheduanna learned the commander's wrong thoughts about adoring at least one God, she felt both surprised and felt happy. It was certain that he wouldn't be among the ones to resist her. She filled in the commander's glass with the pitcher. Meanwhile,Amare whispered something in her ear. She moved towards the depots when she saw that Enheduanna confirmed her nodding. Enheduanna looked at the commander wishing that the conversation should continue:

"You continue surprising me, commander. You are a very interesting person. I wonder what more I will learn about you." she said.

The commander took one more sip from his glass. He tore a piece of the fried mutton from the dish, dried the leaking oil putting against the dish and continued speaking showing the mutton to Enheduanna.

"About the Gods, my princess?"

He threw the meat into his mouth, swallowed it at the first bite and cleaned his hand licking.

"This delicious meat had been in front of them for a long time, as usual none of them touched it and we had a great feast eating this meat, didn't we?"

Enheduanna felt that he was not an ordinary soldier but also knew thinking and questioning in addition to being a dangler and wine addicted man. She had always loved the men who could use their brains but felt nervous if he were a soldier. The only thing she felt happy about him that he would never resist her.

"Commander, you had chosen a wrong career. You should have been a priest or teacher."

He raised his glass toward her sending a loud laughter.

"If I had been one of those, I would have been possibly lying two meters down the earth, head chopped off without breathing., my princess but being a soldier, I could drink and make love without any stop. said he and continued laughing."

Enheduanna joined his laughter, too. She looked into his eyes holding his hands. She responded wearing her usual, charming and joyful smile on her lips and mimics.

"You can continue drinking and making love without any stop as long as you respect," commander.

Namtar stood up pushing his chair back. He bent gently raising his glass towards Enheduanna.

"If I am protecting you and your temple, you should be sure my princess that I respect your belief and please know that my obedience to you is much more than my respect."

Enheduanna raised her glass towards him for his gesture and words.

"It is great to know this, commander, thank you."

She took a few sips from her wine. She let Nakurtum to leave when he asked permission to go for checking the delivery.

Nakurtum wanted to finish the tasks of the night but she also wanted to know where Amare had gone and the interesting note sent to her. She visited the delivery tables hurriedly. The last guests of the night were waiting joyfully for the products they would be given, the priests were carefully delivering and taking their notes. She looked around to see Amare. there were no one else around except the 15-20 persons drinking and enjoying at the tables and the ones waiting for the products. She checked Enheduanna's table last. She was still talking to the commander and they were still drinking but Amare hadn't returned there, either.

While she was hardly walking on this road towards the depot of blankets and clothes, through the small gardens in the back of the temple, dimly lit by the light, she hoped to find Amare but she saw two shadows on the ground, under the tree and about fifteen meters ahead. She shouted:

"Hey, who are you and what are you doing there?" When the two shadows heard her voice, they started running the opposite. Nakurtum felt more doubtful and she felt one more shadow when she came closer to the tree. She started to fear. Her heart was beating so fast. Her hands and feet started shaking. She slowed down. She went on walking bending softly. A few meters to the tree, she saw a woman lying on her right side.

'For the love of Inanna! what's happened here?" she whispered to herself and reached the woman. She turned her on her back. She couldn't see her face clearly as it was dark. She felt that her hands touched a warm liquid thing.

Damn it, It is blood!" she shouted and ran back where she had passed through. She shouted at the priests working in the depots.

"Come here, come here at once and bring a few firebrands!"

Three priests hearing Nakurtum ran to her getting firebrands. Nakurtum, out of breath, shaking in fear, excitement, feeling as if her heart beating suppressing her own voice and someone was drowning her screamed:

"there, There, There is a wounded woman under the tree!"

The priests ran to the tree at once. Nakurtum joined them, too. When they reached there, she saw that the woman was Amare. Tears started running down her cheeks. She knelt down. After a time, her crying turned into sobbing. She collapsed on Amare. She started cleaning her face off the blood and shook the unmoving body screaming in a crying tone:

"My amare, Amare, my beautiful nun, my comrade! Open your eyes, please! What's happened to you?"

One of the priests held his hand to her mouth and nose to see if she could breathe. then he put his head on her chest and listened for about 15-20 seconds if her heart was beating or not.

"Priestess, do not go further please, she had already died. There is nothing we could do."

She was still sobbing. The priest checking Amare talked to the priest standing behind.

"Go and inform the Holy Sister about the case. Never tell anyone else. Then come back here."

The priest ran away. He slowed down to avoid realization when he reached the great garden in which the ceremonies had been made. When she reached Enheduanna, he saw that she was drinking wine and talking with the city guard Namtar. He slowly approached her and whispered into her ear.

"We have a very important problem, my Holy Sister."

The oftenest thing Enheduanna had heard in this short night was the nervous voice saying: "We have got a problem!" What else had happened except the God statues being broken? She was out of taste any more. It was very clear from her frowning, falling face, her stern and short words.

"What, what's happened again?"

"We have found the priestess Amare in the small rear garden, I think, she had been killed." he said.

Enheduanna hearing him stood up immediately and started running towards the rear garden.

She reached the tree. She stood still on the head side of Amare. She knelt down and put Amare's head on her knees and caressing her hair. She couldn't prevent her tears no matter how hard she tried not to cry but be strong. Her tears rushing down started to drop on Amare's face down Enheduanna's face. The commander Namtar coming after her knelt near her, too. He pressed his two fingers of the right hand on Amare's neck and waited for a few seconds.

"Unfortunately, she had died, my Holy Sister." he said.

He stood up and helped Enheduanna to stand up holding her arms. Enheduanna continued crying for a time leaning her head on his shoulder. Namtar spoke to Nakurtum:

"Priestess Nakurtum, please stand up, don't tire yourself in vain. Take the Holy Sister to her room. I care the rest."

Nakurtum stood up and helped Enheduanna go to her room through the back door of the temple.

Namtar told the priest near him:

"Get the corpse and follow me." He headed towards the altars through the back door. When they reached the altar of Inanna, he wanted them to leave it there. In a stern and absolute voice, he warned and left the area:

"Wait here, never let anyone in, never leave the corpse and never tell anything to anyone!"

Enheduanna trying to feel calm washing her hands and face with Nakurtum's help after reaching her room started to feel fine but it was very clear that she was psychologically down. She had witnessed the death of a close person to her for the first time. She had lost her mother before but she couldn't have anything on her mind about her as she was so small as a baby. Whenever she tried to hold herself, she remembered Amare's face and her thin, childish voice and she was sobbing again. Nakurtum was no different than her. Enheduanna, in a moaning and crying tone, said:

"My beautiful nun, please tell priest Akiya that he must accompany and check the celebrations and make the products delivery under his control."

She cleaned her running nose using the skirt of her cloth and added:

"Never tell him anything, no one should hear it. If they ask about me, tell them that I was a little drunk and you took me to my room. The celebrations must continue and people should finish enjoying and then go to their homes. After that, you come back to me and bring some wine please."

Nakurtum was still under shock. She was in fear even while walking in the deserted temple lit by fire-brands and oil candles. She felt that she would en-counter something immediately or someone may attack her behind. She came to the great garden constantly looking back and in strides. The remaining guests were still drinking, dancing and enjoying with-out being aware of anything. She went to the rear area where the priests were sitting. She looked for the priest Akiya. She hardly found him through the crowd. She went closer to him.

"The priest Akiya, the Holy Sister wants you to con-trol the delivery of the cereal, She won't be able to join this time, please get ready after the ceremony. The priests finished the delivery plan. You will only keep the list of what has been given and to whom. I will make the depot counting tomorrow by myself."

The old Akiya was not pleased what he had heard.

"This old Akiya had never felt easy in this temple, ok the priestess Nakurtum, I will be there." he said.

Nakurtum went to the table Enheduanna had sat, got the wine pitcher and the two glasses and came back to the room of the Holy Sister through the road in quick and short steps like her fast beating heart, looking back through the darkness, as if two eyes or feet were coming after her.

When Nakurtum entered the room, Enheduanna was still crying silently. The tears falling down from her large, hazel eyes to her nose, to her firm and crimson lips, to her jaw and then to her hands she put on her knees. She set the pitcher and the glasses near the sofa. She immediately opened the box and took out a cloth that they used as scarf. She dried her eyes, face and hands. She put her right hand on her shoulder sitting next to her. She pulled her gently towards her and leaned her on her shoulder.

After they cried together and then felt calm, Enheduanna spoiled the silence and the sorrowful mood.

"I still can't believe, how and why in the world such a thing could happen? Who could do it? And in the temple?"

Nakurtum dried her hands and face again after wetting it in a pitcher. She was thinking what to say. She had so many things to tell but she couldn't know it this was a proper time.

"In the end, the murderers would be found and punished, my Holy Sister, don't worry, Amare will not be a dead end."

"Do you know where she is now? I hope that poor girl isn't still under the tree."

"I heard that the commander Namtar ordered it to be taken to the altar. right after us. I think she is in the hall where the altars were situated."

"I want to examine Amare with the healers after the ceremonies. I want to know how she was killed."

"The celebrations were about to be over. We can go down slowly to the altars if you want. I will fetch the healers before they went to their homes."

"O, daughter, I am ready, we can't gain anything crying or feeling sorry. We could have been in Amare's shoes. My beautiful Amare. She must be watching us from her palace in Inanna's arms." she said and sat up.

She took off her clothes and wore another one that she took out of the box. Nakurtum was watching her, too. She couldn't take her eyes away from her perfect body.

they came down to the area where the altars were situated. There were three priests waiting near the corpse. Nakurtum spoke to the youngest one:

"Fetch the healer priests and priestesses," She turned to the other priests:

"Please, you wait outside, wait there till we call you, never let anyone in." she said.

Enheduanna took off Amare's clothes carefully. Some parts of the clothes had been stuck her body as the blood there had been clotted. She put the cloth she had taken off on the bansur near. AMare was lying lifeless fully naked on the altar. She looked into her eyes. They were still open and it could be deduced that there was a surprise at her glances. It was clear that she hadn't expected such an end. Enheduanna wanted water to be able to see her wounds better. She cleaned her wounds dropping the large pitcher of water slowly Nakurtum had brought on to her lifeless body. She cleared the blood clots on the ground scratching with her nails, too. Meanwhile, Nakurtum searched her pocket, took out the tablet and then put in her own pocket.

The mortal wounds that she had taken became clearer when her body was cleaned. One wound was just on her heart and the other was on her neck. The wound on her neck was so deep that the neck was about to chop. While Enheduanna and Nakurtum examined Amare, the healer priest and priestess came, too. they understood what was going on and started examining the corpse. The healer priestess inserted her fourth finger into the wound on the heart and took it out. She turned to Enheduanna and said:

"My Holy Sister, I must open the wound so I could tell you about the size of the knife used."

Enheduanna nodded in confirmation. The healer priestess took a small, sharp edged knife and made small cuts round the wound down to the bottom. She measured the depth and height of the wound with the small stick she took out of her bag. She performed the same measurements on the wound of her neck, too. She wrote a few things on a tablet. She wrote the measurements on it, too and handed out to the Holy Sister. Enheduanna examined the tablet for a time.

"As far as I have seen, there is no sign of struggle. What do you think?"

"You are right, the Sister, there are a few small bruises but they are not the type could happen in a struggle. I see a few smashes on her wrists. It is possible that they had try to drag the corpse holding her wrists after they had killed." said the priestess. Then, Enheduanna ordered at the priests waiting outside:

She told them to go to the tree and never let anyone approach it. Then she turned back to the healer priestess:

"Please tell me what else you have realised."

She had asked the question to the priestess but the healer priest interrupted:

108   "My Holy Sister, the first attack had been made to her heart but when she didn't die, her throat was cut off. The knife thrown into her heart can't be the same as the one cutting her throat."

Enheduanna felt surprised what she heard.

"Please go ahead, how did you understand it?"

"My lady, I was a soldier before. I used both knives and swords in the wars. I saw what kinds of wounds a knife or a sword could make. The wound on her neck was starting from one side to the other and it is quite deep. You can't make this wound with the knife thrown to her heart. It is impossible, only a sword can do this."

Enheduanna felt more surprised. After thinking for a while:

"You say that there are two murderers, don't you, the priest?"

"No, the Holy Sister, a person can carry both a knife and a sword."

As soon as he finished his words, Nakurtum jumped:

"My Holy Sister, I had seen them."

Enheduanna felt curious:

"How did you see, my daughter, why don't you tell us?"

"I had gone to check the delivery preparations in the depots. I couldn't find the priest Endugagga responsible for them. I was going through the rear gardens towards the buildings where the blankets and the clothes were stored to look for Amare, I saw moving shadows under the tree in the middle of the garden. I spoke to them, as soon as the shadows heard my voice, turned back and ran away. Then I approached the tree and found Amare's corpse."

"Couldn't you see who they were?"

"No, my Holy Sister because it was dark. They were at the same height but one of them was running faster than the other because that one quickly disappeared despite the two starting two run at the same time. The other disappeared later."

Enheduanna listening to her attentively felt in deep thoughts. She was animating the things having happened in her mind.

The ceremonies in the great garden had ended, the product delivery had started and there were a few persons waiting in the queue. Each person was getting what was his/her share, setting out for their homes with the candles in their hands and disappearing. No one knew what was going on.

Enheduanna spoke to the priests waiting in the back:

"Fetch me the priest Endugagga and commander Namtar at once. I will be waiting for them both in my room. My priestess, please, make the corpse ready til the morning for the funeral."

The healer priestess bent her head to show her pleasure:

"Your orders, my Holy Sister."

Enheduanna put her arm into Nakurtum's arm and headed towards the garden where the murder had been made getting a firebrand from the altar leading the yard. There was a priest following them. When they reached the tree, Enheduanna held down the firebrand and started examine the place Amare was killed on. The grass was still crushed. When she looked back, the grass starting from the temple wall to the tree had been crushed. Then she started examining the path where the murderers had escaped. She was carefully stepping on the grass. She gestured the others to follow her. After taking a few steps, she stopped and crouched on the ground. She held the firebrand low above the ground. She asked the priest whom she wanted to stay there:

"Have you walked up here before?"

"No, my lady, I have waited near the tree all the time."

"Then, bring a few tree branches to me."

The priest broke a tree branch and handed to her breaking it into four pieces. She planted one of them in the sand just before her.

The ones waiting for her standing hadn't realised what she saw. She continued ahead on the same line holding the firebrand low. She was also looking back from time to time. A few steps later, she knelt down and planted one more branch in the sand. They had reached the top wall of the temple after a few steps more. Turning left here could reach the great garden, the side wall and the garden wall was about ten steps of distance.

She realised the blood trace on the temple wall when she was about to hold the firebrand low. She left one branch there, too. She examined the rest of the area slowly. She turned to the priests and said:

"One of you wait here and the other was at the other end till the soldiers have come and never let anyone between the two spots."

She nodded to Nakurtum meaning: let's go! and they went to the study room without speaking. She asked Nakurtum in a pensive mood: Where is my beer, priestess?

Nakurtum bent slightly holding her skirt.

"I had taken it to your bedroom, my Holy Sister. If you want I can fetch one more for you."

When Enheduanna nodded to confirm her, she left the room and started descending the stairs. When she reached the garden story, she saw the commander

Namtar talking to someone foreign. She receded not to be caught and tried to listen what was spoken. She hardly heard the speeches. The commander was speaking in a whisper and the foreign man was making short responses like Yes, I understand ETC.

She went out to the garden thinking that waiting and listening here would do no good. She got the beer pitcher and two glasses on Enheduanna's desk. Then she approached the commander Namtar pretending to realise at the last moment.

"Commander, we can't find you if we wanted to search but you are everywhere when we don't need you." she teased.

"Oh, the priestess Nakurtum, I went to the police station at once, gave the necessary orders and had just come."

"I don't know who the man with you now? I have seen him for the first time, Is she a soldier?"

"No, he is my guest from Uruk. He was about to leave already."

"My Holy Sister has been waiting for you in her room, you had better hurry. Please take these beer pitcher and the glasses, she had requested them."

"My pleasure, priestess Nakurtum."

He nodded to the man he had been speaking as if to say You can leave getting the glasses and the pitcher. Nakurtum had caught this gesture, too.

While the Commander Namtar headed towards Enheduanna's room, Nakurtum hurriedly came to the depot room and held the arm of one of the young priests.

"Do you see this man leaving? She continued when he nodded in confirmation."

"Follow him till his last destination without being notified and learn who he is if possible."

The young priest:

"Your orders, Priest Nakurtum." Then he quickly disappeared through the darkness after the man.

When she approached Enheduanna's room, she didn't enter the door immediately and listened through the door. She was busy with discussing with commander. She was putting forward how the city and especially the temple were risky for attacks.

As today was offer day, the temple was more crowded and harder to be secured than the other days. On special days, the visitors of the temple were not the only Ur people but also from the other cities for just the celebrations. There were also tradesmen coming in their boats and caravans. The commander must be more cautious and attentive than before as being the city guard. It was prohibited that the soldiers could enter the temple in uniforms and armed but there must be patrols at the entrance of the doors and around the temple regularly. Their most important duty was to check the persons entering the temple and to investigate the suspects. It was clear today that something was missed or incomplete.

Enheduanna requested from the commander the list of the people having entered the city for the last two days. there were three doors on the city boundary and all the foreigners entering were registered in a list. This was the routine work of the soldiers.

She said to the commander that the depot in charge Priest Endugagga hadn't been on his duty during the event and he was not around either. She ordered the commander that he be found and investigated; no one must be allowed to leave the city until the event had been settled.

Nakurtum, unable to wait more entered the room knocking at the door. She nodded greeting, passed on the right side of Enheduanna and sat crouching on her knees. She stared at the commander from top to bottom. The shield of his sword caught her eyes. She remembered that His sword was in the shield in the event area but now it was empty. She started speaking to him in implications.

"Commander, I see that you don't have your sword with you in an event that you would need it the most, I hoped you would be more cautious."

The commander paused for a moment, inhaled a few breathes and said looking into her eyes in angry and threatening mood,

"My priestess, never worry, I can use my hands so skilfully as my sword so I didn't need to wear my sword."

Nakurtum felt the implication in his glances and responded showing that she was not afraid:

"I have no worry, commander, I hope you can use your mind as well as your arms."

After her words, he tried to stand up and say unable to hide his anger and in his harsh tone:

"My priestess can directly tell if she wants to say anything but I deny you speak in such implications."

Enheduanna pointed him to sit back.

"Please, there is no point in discussing with each other, while the lifeless body of one of my most obedient priestess Amare was lying on the cold altar. We are all tensed and we have a murder that we have to conclude."

She couldn't help and her eyes felt tears. The commander got permission that his soldiers could enter the temple armed temporarily. He left the temple saying that he would immediately send the documents that Enheduanna wanted.

After the commander had left, Enheduanna and Nakurtum reviewed what had happened by that time and tried to make a conclusion of it. They started drinking slightly from time to time to ease their tense. While Enheduanna was thinking that the only suspect was the Priest Endugagga who hadn't been found despite the search, she added the Commander Namtar and the foreigner he had spoken in the temple garden to the list of suspects after she had spoken to Nakurtum.

As the number of the suspects increased, it was getting harder to conclude the crime but Enheduanna never lost hope that it would be concluded in the end. In the future, everything could change because every murder left the trace of the murderer after the crime.

Nakurtum instantly remembered the tablet she had taken out of Amare's pocket and handed it to enheduanna taking it out. Then she said:

"This tablet had been sent to Amare before the ceremony, my Holy Sister. A man had given it to one of the priestesses. I asked her about the identity of the man, she said that she hadn't known him and his face was covered by a veil. She had brought it to me for Amare. I don't know what it read but Amare left the table after reading it and everything happened after it."

Enheduanna got the small tablet and started reading it. Nakurtum feeling curious asked her what it read. The Holy Sister started to read each word carefully and trying to understand the meanings of them.

"The flock had entered the barn, don't cook the food, the dog of the shepherd is lying under the same tree." What could it mean? she asked.

Nakurtum couldn't get any meanings from the words, either. they caught each others eyes instantly. Nakurtum, getting the tablet out of her hand and examining it for a while started to speak excitedly:

"My Holy Sister, I think, it wants to imply the meeting place when it mentioned "The dog of the shepherd is lying under the same tree." Amare had been killed under the tree."

And Enheduanna interrupted her words and continued speaking:

"And the murderer of Amare is the shepherd's dog, that's not the real murderer, only a man of the murderer."

"I am in the same opinion, my lady. Even if we found the murderer, we had to find the real one behind him."

"But what it could mean by: "the flock entered the room and don't cook the food?""

The real question confusing Nakurtum was this and may be these words could be the ones to shed light on the murder and conclude it. But no matter how hard she tried, she couldn't get anything out of these words.

"I have no idea, my Holy Sister, but pay attention please, there is a small crack in the middle of the reed pencil used. There is an emboss among the characters."

"Yes, I have seen it now, It is certain that a cracked pencil was used for this writing and we could find the writer of this tablet if we could find the pencil."

"Don't worry my Holy Sister, I will do my best."

Enheduanna had forgotten an important task out of control while she was dealing with this murder. Nakurtum had realised that the Holy Sister had forgotten her previous plans out of her control. She didn't want to distract her attention mentioning her about it but no matter what it was, the order of the God must be performed. What she head learned in the temple for years that God never wanted anything from humans but if something was demanded via a holy person, it must certainly be performed, otherwise they could be flooded away like the people of Ziudsura disobeying their God.

When she saw that Enheduanna was opening the bottom drawer of the cabinet in which she put her tablets on the right side of her door in her room, she understood that a magic session would be held soon. She left the room getting permission to leave her alone and complete her tasks.

Enheduanna got the tablet on which human pictures were drawn and the plate in which she always made fumigation and set them on the table. She got a semen pegani, four or five bayleaves and a sharp stick made of cypress from the bottom drawer of the cabinet and returned to her table. First, she poured the semen pegani and the bayleaves into the fumigation plate and then lit the seeds using the candle oil on the opposite wall. The room started to fill up a thin fog and a dizzying, throat burning odour. Enheduanna, taking the tablet in one hand and the sharp edged stick into another hand started to read the magic pray pressing the sharp edge on some spots of the man picture on the tablet:

"Oh, the destroyer of all the bad and the owner of the burning flames of the hell, Inanna! accept my pray with the sharp odour rising out of my fumigation and help my damn come true! Those who took the Priestess Amare who was under my order should have broken generations, decayed hands, blind eyes, non walking feet, non smelling noses, be in pieces like this tablet and no one should recognise them." She stood up and thrown the tablet through the window.

Seconds later, the tablet hit the stone ground and scattered into pieces. Enheduanna inhaling the fume in the room and lying on the sofa felt slightly dizzy and her soul was forced out of her body. The tiredness of the day and the fume had impacted her. She lost her conscious. there were white clouds passing by her eyes. After a time, the Queen of the Heavens smiled at her through the clouds. Next to her, Amare in pure white clothes and under a golden and diamond crown was shaking her hands as it to say that she was with her, too. She blinked her eyes but the same picture was before her eyes. She didn't feel the bottom parts of her body. She wanted to move her hands but couldn't whereas her whole body still existed. All the signs of her humanity started leave her one by one. She felt so easy as a bird's wing when she left her own body. Her body was lying on the bed.

She watched herself for a time. She thought that she had died but she didn't feel any heart beatings or excitements that she had when she was in fears. She was very peaceful and at ease.

She raised her head when the heavy illumination cloud surrendered her. The source of the light was a door consisted of different pieces. She started to be pulled into this door quickly and passed through it slowly. She understood that the illumination and the door she had gone through was herself. There were colorful houses made of mosaic glasses and crystal people. The bird like transparent livings with wings were flying around.After a time, she started lowering through the illumination. She passed back through the same dor and she found herself sleeping by lying on her bed. She opened her eyes, she inhaled the fume out of the semen pegani dancing in the shaking light of the oil candle. She closed her eyelids she can no longer bear and fell a deep sleep.

When Nakurtum went out to the corridor, it was half dark. The oil candles on the ground dimly lit her path. The weak firebrands on the walls gave the corridor a mysterious, magical look. It still bore the pleasant smell of the fumes burned on the day. The candle waves were dancing in the soft breeze of the wind and shedding moving shadows on the walls. While walking, she was feeling that someone was coming after or watching her, she was getting more scared, her heart was beating hard and her steps were turning into strides. Death was all around in the house of Gods and it could be anywhere and anytime. She thought, Fear only pushes towards the death. When she reached the hall where the altars were situated, she looked inside to check if there was anybody there. there was nothing but the poor Amare's lifeless body wrapped up in linen cloth lying on the cold stone.

The altar hall had never been so cool to her before

and it felt mysteriously death. Without waiting much, she went down to the basement where the seclusion rooms were built. She saw the women who weren't selected lying on the sofa in the mid yard. She hoped that Urnina should be there, too. She approached the sleeping women and checked their faces one by one. Urnina wasn't there. She had no idea about which room she was in. At that time, she heard one of the women calling her in her name in a whisper. She was Ahunatum who wanted permission to get married on the public day. As she was still in the hall, it meant that no foreign man had wanted her yet. Nakurtum felt sorry for her misfortune.

'Have you come for someone, Priestess Nakurtum?"

Nakurtum headed towards the bad fortuned girl and whispered to her ear:

"I am looking for the Priestess Urnina."

The woman pointed the no 12 cross room. Nakurtum approached the door thanking her. She listened through the door for a time. She could hear Urnina's moaning and the sounds made by the two bodies when they combined representing the Holy Coupling. She had doubt to enter or not. She went to the section reserved for Urnina to wait for a time. She couldn't realise how much she had waited due to the thoughts rushing through her mind like bees. Her body could no longer bear tiredness and sleeplessness. Her eyeballs were aching, her brain was feeling numb and her patellas were tingling. When she returned to the dor, the only thing she could hear was a man's snoring. She silently opened the door. She approached the bed on her fingers and poked Urnina. She jumped up and sat down in fear. When she saw Nakurtum instantly in the room dimly lit by one oil candle, she couldn't recognise her. She looked ghostly in the weak, gloomy light. Nakurtum held her hand on her mouth and whispered into her ear when she was about to scream.

"Nakurtum, I am the Priestess Nakurtum."

Urnina felt calm after taking deep breathes for a time. She got out of the bed. She wore her sandals and went to the yard after the Priestess Nakurtum. She had forgotten even to take her dress due to her nervousness and drowsiness. She was standing in front of Nakurtum fully naked. Rubbing her eyes:

"For the love of Inanna, Priestess Nakurtum, do you know how late it is? Even the Gods are sleeping at this time." she said.

"I am aware the Priestess Urnina but I didn't have any other choice. Let's not speak here but go up."

The Priestess Urnina went to her room, wore her clothes and headed towards the staircase after Nakurtum. They reached the entrance floor. Nakurtum warned her against the corpse of Amare that she would see a little later. She told her not to scream and grunt. They went inside. Urnina directly went to Amare's corpse. She covered her face when she saw the lifeless face, of Amare like the pale and hard marble stone.

"High of the highs, Inanna, what's happened here?" she could say.

Amare's body had been washed by the Healer

Priestess and covered up by a linen cloth. Her feet side was tied up with a piece of cloth.

The cold face of death had materialised on her beautiful, smooth face and sealed her body as a lifeless corpse.

The Priestess Nakurtum told her what's happened shortly and informed her about the last instruction given by the Holy sister. She wanted her to help her. She promised that she would offer her to the Holy Sister on Amare's behalf. The Priestess Urnina looked at the empty place on her right and left where they were supposed to be the statues of the Gods. She paused for a moment. She looked at Amare's very pale and frozen face. She nodded as if to say, "yes."

Nakurtum sent her to the wards near the depots in which the slaves rested, wanted her to pick four of them up and asked her to bring them where she wanted. Then she headed towards the depots where the blankets and clothes were stored behind the temple. She wanted to go through the left of the entrance as a short cut but then she decided to go around the area where the depots were built so she would have the possibility to check if the priests Enheduanna had placed were still there or not. She came after the Priestess Urnina till the depots. She turned the corner. She found the young priest sleeping near the wall crouched.

She approached him and poked with her feet. "Wake up, the young priest." He couldn't understand at first as he was drowsy. Then he stood up at once when he realised that she were the Priestess Nakurtum. She asked if there were anything worth attention. She continued her way when she learned that things were ok. When she came to the other corner of the temple passing by the tree under which she found Amare's dead, she saw the other priest that they had left there. She greeted him and moved on after asking the same questions and getting positive answers. She came to the depot. She pulled one of the bricks on the top of the door toward herself, got the keys hidden in it and opened the door.

When the Priestess Urnina saw that the four slaves came after her, she felt happy as the things were going on as planned. She would have finished all the things before the sun rise. After she made the slaves wrap the remaining pieces of the statues of Gods in clothes and blankets, she wanted them to carry the pieces to the cars kept near the iron men. After they loaded the pieces carefully in the cars, she made them covered once more. They all returned to the altar when the things were completed. They put the statue of the Goddess Inanna just opposite of the entrance door. They put all the altars in an order in front of it and placed the bansurs on the left and the right sides of the Inanna statue. The only thing remaining was the corpse of Amare that they had laid down. They took it with themselves and went up to the scribe room of Nakurtum.

Nakurtum warning each slave one by one said that the Holy Sister freed themselves. They should be quiet and they would be released tomorrow. The slaves went to their wards feeling happy that they would come together with their wives, children and their countries which they had been away from for ages. The Priestess Nakurtum told the Priestess Urnina that they had only one last thing to do. She said to her that she must return to the seclusion room but before it, she must go to the temple door and tell the soldiers that they mustn't allow anyone in till the Holy Sister ordered and she must lock the door behind.

The Priestess Urnina feeling tired, drowsy, her head bent down and left the temple in short steps to order the things to be done.

Little had left the sun rise. Before the city Ur woke up, she must wake the Holy Sister up and tell her what's happened. There are a lot of things to be done but the tiredness started impacting first from her back to the neck and then to her eyes. She hardly kept her eyes open. She fell a deep sleep out of control near the lifeless body of the Priestess Amare.

The things she had lived on the day affected her personality. She had seen them in her dreams and now she was in the celebrations. She was sitting at the same desk with the Holy Sister and they were eating food.

When Amare called her and said that the nuns weren't there, she paid attention to the matter and started checking around. then, the public would be delivered the weekly products and she wanted to perform this duty. Amare wanted to go to the rear depo to arrange the clothes and the blankets to wrap the statues up. While leaving the Holy Sister together to do their jobs, the Priestess Nakurtum told Amare; "You check the product delivery status, I want to go to the blanket depot because I am fed up with doing the same things all the time." Amare in a warm smile:

"However you want, dear priestess, please be careful." she said and headed towards the depots. Nakurtum turned through the path near the depots and went towards the rear garden. She felt that she remembered here in her dream. Something had happened here. She felt as if something in the deeper part of her brain was waking her up. when she moved slowly through the darkness and approached the middle tree, she felt that two shadows were coming toward her from the temple wall. As the music played in the ceremony was too high, she could hardly hear the voice of one of the men that says: "The Priestess Nakurtum, we had been waiting for you." This voice was very familiar as if it belonged to a man she saw everyday but didn't care. The shadows drew closer. Nakurtum felt a rising fear. Not only her heart but also her forehead was beating fast. One of the shadows approached her and tried to pull her towards the temple wall holding her left arm.

"What are you doing? Let me go! Pull back your hands!" She wanted to scream but couldn't Her tongue could produce no words. When she wanted to speak, the words were hardly coming out but then disappearing through the air and a low grunt was being heard. She felt from the touch of the man that he had been wearing a thick metal ring on his finger because the hand of the man was warm but the coolness of the ring was very clear. The more Nakurtum pulled herself back, the more the man dragged her to the shadowy side of the temple wall. She felt that they were about the same height. The second man appeared through the darkness. That man was taller and larger. His arms were muscled and he was powerful. He held the other arm of her and they dragged her toward the wall. She wanted to say: "What do you want from me?" she wanted to say but the words were never coming out. the short man shouted:

"You will pay for your deception, you dirty whore! and inserted the knife he held in his left hand into her heart."

Nakurtum woke up screaming and sat up breathing fast and in sweat. She put her right hand on her heart, there was nothing wrong. It was all a night mare but what a bad night mare! The things Amare had gone through that day became Nakurtum's dream. She started thinking for a while her eyes fixed on Amare. What a cruel thing to face death while holding on to life closely. She thought of the things Amare might have faced,, she murmured to herself: My dear, poor comrade!"

The first lights of the day started rushing through the window. She stood up and went up to the room of the Holy Sister. The door was still ajar as she had left. When she looked through the door, she saw that the Holy Sister was still sleeping on her sofa. She went inside and closed the door. She touched her shoulder and spoke a few times: "My Holy Sister. enheduanna," hardly awaking sat up rubbing her eyes. She looked at Nakurtum in a painful smile. She held her hand and stood up. She washed her hands and face. She started to look for another dress in the box taking her previous dress off. Meanwhile, Nakurtum was watching the Holy Sister's naked, smooth, pure and charming body. Then, she remembered why Enheduanna wanted to change her dress. She took back the dress she had put on the bed. She inhaled a deep odour of it.

The odour filling in her body had charmed her. The skin odour had been mixed with it and they were both absorbed by the dress. While she was checking the dress, the dry traces of blood on the front side of the dress attracted her attention. In an excited tone,

"My Holy Sister, I think, I have found how to find out the murderer!" she said.

Enheduanna felt excited of what she had heard and asked the expected question:

"How?"

Nakurtum started telling at once, meanwhile, enheduanna was wearing her clothes.

"If there left blood traces on your clothes, the murderers should have the same, too. Do you remember that the Commander Namtar said that he had to change his clothes when I asked him about his sword. In my opinion, he must be your first suspect." she said self assuredly.

Enheduanna listening to her attentively:

"Dear priestess, I know that you don't like Namtar but we mustn't jump into the matter directly. If we judge a person without having any clues, we can loose our chance to find the real murderer." she said emphasising that they must be careful.

Nakurtum nodded her head in confirmation. When the Holy Sister finished dressing, preparation and sat on the bed, Nakurtum told her what had happened till the morning when she was asleep. Enheduanna, feeling emotional against what she had heard, she had forgotten what she must do because of the complications.

"You are a sun shedding more light each day, dear Nakurtum. Thank you very much. I had forgotten them as I was busy with Amare's death. Unfortunately, the pain of death is felt only in the heart like the pain of love not in physics. The pain of my heart had impacted my brain."

Nakurtum feeling proud and little shy said:

"I am the assistant, comrade and servant of the moon faced Holy Sister of the Moon Goddess Inanna, my passionate feelings for you can make me do everything for you, I am willing even to die for you, my dear Holy Sister."

Enheduanna hugged Nakurtum and pulled toward her holding her belly. She kissed her neck and whispered:

"Belief drags someone towards itself. I se that you are one of the most believing me because you are always on my side."

She touched Nakurtum's face and caressed it. They were both aware that today would be a very tiring and problematic day. They made a short plan together. The first thing Enheduanna wanted was to take the samples of the blood traces of the footsteps in the rear garden and the bloody hand prints on the wall. Then the foreigners in the list that the commander would ring would be investigated and the damn Priest Endugagga could be found no matter where he had been hidden. Meanwhile, Nakurtum told her that when she went to the celebration garden to fetch beer, she had sent out a man to follow the foreign man that the commander had been talking and she hoped he would return important information.

they remembered that the doors had been locked. Nakurtum went to open the doors thinking that it wouldn't be good to keep the tens of persons to enter the temple for daily routines. Enheduanna, as she did every morning knelt down in front of the Inanna statue in her room to make her daily pray:

Oh, the Holy Inanna,
What you order should be my life destiny
Even if I had a bad fortune,
I want your blessings, blessings
My whole life is yours
And it will be forever
Your heart is a heaven,
Your blessing is my gift
My failure is my punishment
Enheduanna be the your sacrifice in your holy path

After finishing her pray, She wrote the hair tablet the pray she had just read using her reed pencil sitting on the sofa near the window. After she finished writing, she placed it near the other pray tablets carefully and went down to her other room to carry out her usual tasks.

When enheduanna came back to her room, she found the Commander Namtar and Nakurtum had been waiting for her. She sat the opposite and asked for the recent news. Nakurtum presented the city come in/exit data with her.

I examined the list the Holy Sister, I didn't encountered any suspected entries. The listed names are the tradesmen entering our city. They hadn't had any inconsistencies before..

Enheduanna got the tablets in front of her and put on the cushion on her right. She turned to the commander:

"I want them all in the hall accompanied with you an hour later. I will question them one by one." she said.

The commander listening to her felt nervous.

"My Holy Sister, these people are foreigners, the situation they will be exposed to make take away from our countries preventing them coming back to our country again."

Enheduanna got angry with what she had heard. She threw a hard, frowny and half closed eyes glance at the commander.

"The life of a person in my country is more than the products of tradesmen, commander. It feels more important if the murderer person were the assistant of the Holy Sister of the temple. Don't wait, bring them up all here, include their boxes in which they put their clothes. Check them carefully while they packed their belongings." She said ending her conversation with Namtar.

Namtar felt tensed and had a deep disappointment as he hadn't been favored. He went out of the room showing his disappointment to Enheduanna. Nakurtum said:

"I sent the best sculpturers and picture drawers of the temple to the rear garden, my Holy Sister. They will emboss and draw the traces of the foot prints and the bloods. Then they will bring them to you." she said.

"You are great, Nakurtum. Any word from the Priest Endugagga?"

"The soldiers are searching for him everywhere in and around the temple. I gave the keys of the locked areas. they would check everywhere."

She nodded at Nakurtum in pleasure. There were people waiting in the hall coming for the public day and telling Enheduanna about their problems and desires. The heavy noise coming from indicated that they were a large crowd.

"Tell the people waiting outside that there would be no public day today. Inform them that we have extra ordinary things today, they should come tomorrow."

Nakurtum, receiving the order went out to perform it. She sent everybody to home or their works. there was only one person left in the hall attracting her attention. She spoke to him:

"Sir, haven't you heard, you should come tomorrow."

The man walked toward her instead of responding. He stood just before her and whispered:

"I am Priest Abram. You ordered me to follow a man." She looked at the man more carefully when she heard him. She had forgotten to look at his face yesterday as it was too complicated and busy. She couldn't remember him.

"Yes, I have remembered you but couldn't recognise you as you are civil now. YOu know that it is a big crime, you must walk around in your priest clothes."

"Yes, the Priestess Nakurtum. I had to change my clothes in order to avoid being recognised."

She invited the man into Enheduanna's room. They went inside together. Nakurtum introduced the man to Enheduanna and they started to listen to the man together.

"I started following the man after leaving the temple. A few streets passing, I realised that the man understood to be tracked and I hid myself somewhere watching where he was heading. I went after him street by street. He entered last the tavern of Semiramis. I would have attracted his attention if I had entered inside in my current clothes. I went back at once and I changed my clothes, I put on a cap on my head and returned to the tavern. He had been still there when I entered the tavern. He was talking to someone else at the deserted desk on the left corner of the tavern and they were drinking beer. The man he had been talking was a foreigner. I hadn't seen him in Ur before. Then, they invited one of the girls working in the tavern. the entertained and drank with the girl for a long time. the man I was following became fully drunk. He stood up and headed towards the door. the other man was still at the desk with the girl. I stood up at once and went after him. There was a twenty-step distance between us. He hardly walked. He jerked and fell on the ground at a moment. I thought I had found the opportunity and helped the man stand up. I told him: Let me help you till you would reach your destination, otherwise you can't find it even if you walked at this rate till the morning. The man showed his thanks holding my hand. I asked him while walking. It was Pushu Ken. He had come to Ur three days ago. He was the guest of the commander. I took him to the quarter. I helped him up to the room of the Commander Namtar and lie on his bed. I took off his shoes and clothes. A soldier helped me, too.

Enheduanna interrupted:

"Isn't the commander at the quarter at that time?"

"No, he isn't, my Holy Sister, at least not in the bedroom, but he could be in the study room, I don't know.

Nakurtum interrupted as well:

"Have you ever seen the old clothes of the commander in the room?"

"Yes the Holy Sister, the commander's uniform was on the bed before I lay the man. They were carelessly piled up. I got them and pushed it towards the under of the bed. then, I lay the man and got out of the quarter."

Enheduanna asked him to continue:

"After the quarter, I returned to the tavern of Semiramis. The man had been sitting at the same desk with the same girl. He was drinking beer, kidding with the girl and entertaining with her. I waited till he stood up. A time later, he got out of the tavern, too. I started following him. I returned to the tavern when he entered the guest house for foreign people on the river lake. I returned to the tavern and sat at the same desk. I called the same girl and I ordered a beer for her and one for me. After establishing a relation with the girl, I asked her about the men she had sat before me. One of them came from Elam, he was a weapon trader. She said that she didn't know anything about the man whose name was Pushu Ken. They generally talked about money. Something interesting happened while I talked to the girl. The Priest Akiya entered the tavern. I tried to hide behind the girl to prevent him from seeing me. He asked something to the owner of the tavern Samiramis and left. I paid for the bill immediately and tried to catch him up. But I couldn't find him as he had disappeared through the darkness. I returned home and fell asleep. I came here as soon as I got up, my lady."

Enheduanna stood up, reaching her wooden box on the table and getting five silver coins out of it handed them to him.

"Very well, my priest, you have done a great job. Thank you, these are for your efforts and expenses. Please get them." she said and sat down.

When Nakurtum nodded him to leave, the priest left the room. Enheduanna told Nakurtum to fetch the Priest Akiya and when he reached this room, she must go and check his room in case she could find anything suspected.

Nakurtum quickly headed towards the room of akiya he used for his work. She encountered the Healer Priestess on the road, The priestess asked when the funeral would be made. Nakurtum said that she didn't know saying that she would ask the Holy Sister about it and went on walking. She reached the room of the Priest Akiya. She knocked at the door and entered. The room was empty. After checking outside carefully, she started examining the inside of the room. She looked everywhere she could think of such as under the bed, the cabinet in which the tablets were placed and under the study desk. Nothing looked suspicious. She got out of the room and headed toward Enheduanna's room but she heard sounds at the main entrance of the temple. She turned that side. She saw two soldiers were trying to force the Priest Endugagga, speaking hard words on him. The priest were constantly murmuring, resisting the soldiers and saying that he didn't do anything.

She waited till the soldiers reached her and they went to the room of the Holy Sister's room. The soldiers pushed him to the room by force and started waiting in front of the door to prevent him from escaping. Nakurtum sat on the cushions on the right of enheduanna removing the tablets behind.

The Priest Endugagga in a very desperate situation. All around him was covered by sand and his clothes were in vomit. He was waiting hands tied and head bent.

Enheduanna:

"We have been searching for you since yesterday night, you have been nowhere." One of the soldiers responded before the priest:

"My Holy Sister, we have found this man sleeping among the back sacks in cereal depots. There were three wine pitchers with him."

"Where have you been, priest, tell me!" shouted Enheduanna.

The Priest Endugagga responded in sorrowful, crying and shy tone:

"My lady, I didn't do any wrong. I swear to all the Gods and the morning star rising before the morning sun. I got wines with me during the celebrations, hid myself behind the depot to prevent the people from seeing me and drank them. Then I fell a deep sleep. The soldiers came and woke me up."

"The Priest Akiya had to make the delivery on your behalf. You left your job and drank beer despite knowing that drinking at work hours was prohibited. It is nearly the noon and you are still not at your work. I dismiss you from your duty of temple priest and damn you for the sake of the Goddess Inanna. I punished you in the prison forever till the Goddess ordered you to be sent out. Then, you will be dismissed from the lands of Inanna forever! Get this man and sent to the prison!"

Enheduanna pointed to the soldiers and they took him out carrying in their arms. Endugagga was crying in screams and begging for mercy but Enheduanna didn't care him. Nakurtum asked permission to check the picture drawers and the sculpturers working in the garden, organize the funeral of Amare ad left the room after the soldiers. She came back to the room and informed Enheduanna when she saw the commander, soldiers and the foreign traders. Enheduanna wanted them to wait in the hall till the sculpturers finished their work. Nakurtum informed them about Enheduanna's order and went out to the garden. She felt happy when she saw the picture drawers and sculpturers were about to finish their work. She told them to go to the room of the Holy Sister and passed to the Healer Priestess. She told her that the funeral would be made tomorrow and ordered that the corpse must be taken to one of the cooler seclusion rooms from the area in which the altars were situated. She asked her if she had seen the Priest Akiya or not. When she learned his whereabout, she headed towards the laundry room.

The Priest Akiya was hanging his washed clothes but today wasn't a washing day. No washing was made unless an emergency occurred. Before he saw her, she quickly got out of the laundry and started waiting near the kitchens. After a time, the Priest Akiya got

138

out of the laundry and met Nakurtum near the kitchen while he was going towards the temple. Nakurtum directly asked with a stern voice:

"The Holy Sister has been looking for you since the morning, you must visit her right now."

Nakurtum interrupted him when he was about to say something:

"I told you what you had to do, priest Akiya, please don't ask any questions, just do what you were ordered."

While the Priest akiya was going towards Enheduanna's room bent down and worried, Nakurtum returned to the laundry. She checked the clothes that Akiya left for dry. If the blood had been on the clothes, she could have seen traces of it but she couldn't find anything and headed towards Enheduanna's room. Then she remembered that the voice of the murderer speaking in her dream that she had in the morning was just like his voice. He was in this murder but she couldn't proove it like she couldn't prove the commander's guilt.

She returned to Enheduanna's room without wasting time. When she entered the room, she saw that the sculpturers and the picture drawer were in the room. They had the haired samples of the foot prints and the blood traces on the wall. They told her how they replicated the exact footsteps and traces. Enheduanna had ordered them to be brought over heating and hardened and a lot of softened new hairs. After they left the room, the Priest Akiya waiting outside entered the room. He had a shy and bent down mood as usual.

"You have ordered me, the Holy sister, I am at your service." he said showing his respect."

Enheduanna directly spoke:

"You made the delivery by yourself right after the ceremony last night, didn't you?"

"Yes, my Holy Sister, you had ordered so."

"I wonder what you did after the delivery, may I learn it?"

"Of course, my Holy Sister. I went back to my home and got rest.

Till the morning, the priest Akiya?"

"Yes, my Holy Sister, till the sun rise, then I came to the temple to do my work."

"Someone had seen you in the tavern of Semiramis at night. Are they likely to see that they had seen a man resembling you?"

The Priest Akiya paused for a moment, he choked, weighed on his mind what to say and understood that he didn't have enough time to think.

"Yes, the Holy Sister, I had wanted to calm down drinking somethings before going home. I had to leave the tavern when the owner woman said that they were about to close."

When the Priest Akiya had finished his words, Nakurtum and Enheduanna caught each others eyes, they were thinking the same thing. Enheduanna turned to the Priest Akiya:

"Thank you Priest Akiya, please bring the Priest Abram here. I want you both here." she said.

He left the room bending his head down and moving backward. He couldn't understand how the Holy Sister could learn all those things. He hadn't seen any familiar persons when he went to the tavern at that night. Either Enheduanna was bluffing or she was really aware of everything. He had understood from her words that he was about to end up. He thought that he didn't have much things to do. He decided that the only way was to escape. But how? All the doors of the city were closed and all incomings or outgoings were prohibited. His psychology had reflected on his face so much that those who saw him could think that he was no different than a dead. He exited through the door of the temple and disappeared in Ur.

The commander came after the Priest Akiya but Enheduanna waved him to leave. He instantly left the room. They waited thinking in a remarkable long time and a deep silence till the door was knocked. When Enheduanna ordered them to enter, the sculpturer and the picture drawer appeared in front of her. They had hardened the footprints, the blood traces and brought the new soft hair balls.

She ordered the drawer and the sculpturer to sit near the cross wall.

She ordered Nakurtum to let the commander and the first trader in. She questioned all the traders one by one from where they came to where they were in the evening of the celebrations. They generally gave the same answers. That was the natural result of their staying at the same guest room and meeting each other from time to time. The data about the incoming and outgoing foreigners was compatible with the persons in question.

After the last trader left, Nakurtum warn Enheduanna that the weapon trader and the man called Pushu Ken that the Priest Abra mentioned were not here. Enheduanna had realised this fact as well.

"Commander, two of the names of the two persons weren't listed here, the one was your guest Pushu Ken and the other was the friend of your guest-the Elam trader."

The commander's jaw dropped when he heard this question. It was impossible that she knew these people were in the city. Then, he remembered that Nakurtum had seen him talking to Pushu Ken at the end of the celebration day but it was impossible that she knew his name. After thinking so many things in seconds,

"My Holy Sister, as Pushu Ken was my personal guest, I myself let in the boundary door. I didn't need to register him but I don't have any information about the man whom you said to be an Elam trader." he said half ignoring the question.

Enheduanna had never been satisfied by the answers of the commander because she had demanded all the foreigners not only the traders. in the city.

"Commander, you have half an hour, you will fetch these two foreigners to me otherwise, I wouldn't be responsible what would be the next."

Enheduanna clearly and seriously threatened the

commander. The commander stood up, left the room in quick and nervous steps.

Despite the Priest Akiya searching for the Priest Abram for a long time, he hadn't been able to find him yet in the temple. It was a very hard task. Enheduanna and Nakurtum were thinking the same things but they were afraid to express their worries. What if if one of the guilty persons was the Priest Akiya and were busy with escaping? The doors had been closed and no one was allowed out or in. There was nowhere he could go. They weighed their options when they were alone. There were four suspects and they were all connected with each other. Pushu Ken, he was the man whom he met in the tavern and he was connected with the commander. The Priest Akiya was connected with Pushu Ken and the weapon trader. It was possible that he couldn't meet them as he had to make the product delivery. It was almost certain 143 that he had gone there to meet them. There were two murderers and four suspects. A period later, the commander came with his soldiers and one more man seemed to be brought by force.

"My Holy Sister, this is the man you know as Elam weapon trader. We couldn't find him in the guest houses and the taverns around but the soldiers had caught him while he was trying to escape a short time before."

"Congratulations on you, commander, What a nice thing it is that your soldiers could cover you up but I feel that two more persons must be caught as well. As far as I see, your guest isn't with you now."

"I am sure he is in the city. We will find him soon,

too."

Enheduanna turning to the foreigner hand and feet tied among the soldiers asked:

"What is your name, how long have you been here?"

The man responded Enheduanna rudely without even looking at her face:

"If you don't know who I am, why have you made me brought here?"

"How do you know the man called Pushu Ken, where is he now?"

Elam man without turning his head away from the right side, insisting on his rude, hatred and proud glances,

"WE were making love with the same Ur woman, how shouldn't I know him? How can I know where he is, if you can't know." he said.

Enheduanna, feeling his smarty and unnecessary answers pointed to the commander. The commander grabbed his hair, pulled it back and fisted on his throat. The man bent down on his knees as if to drown. He put his head on the ground and grunted as if he were about to die of chokes. The commander held his hair again and pulled up to make him sit on his knees. Enheduanna was used to seeing such things when she was growing up near her father. She wasn't affected by that scene that much but Nakurtum had never experienced such torture events before. She felt little uneasy and also her stomach had run. Enheduanna, in a firmer tone, said to Elam man:

"Asking you for the last time, who are you, why are you here and how do you know Pushu Ken?"

The commander's efforts were in vain. The man was no longer speaking rudely but he was not speaking at all, either. There was nothing much to do any more. Enheduanna order his foot and hand prints embossed on the hair surface. The soldiers and Namtar could manage to get the prints after long efforts and tries. Nakurtum took the soft hairs on which the prints were made for dry at once. When she returned, she saw that the commander was talking to a soldier in front of the door of Enheduanna. She approached them.

"I hope it is about the searched suspects, commander Namtar?"

The commander returned to Nakurtum after giving a few commands to the soldier.

"Yes priestess, they have found the priest Akiya but his lifeless body."

Nakurtum was in a surprised and nervous mood. The man they had suspected the most was dead now. Unfortunately, deads couldn't tell much. They went to the room. The Commander informed Enheduanna about what had happened. He said that the Priest Akiya was found dead throat cut in the three sub street behind the temple. The soldiers were going to bring his corpse to the temple soon.

Enheduanna could sense what had happened. The Priest Akiya had felt that the Holy Sister was about to settle the matter and little time left for his arrest. He wanted help from Pushu Ken to be able to tell him about the situation and escape but the priest had forgotten this: no murderer carried the clues with themselves. He quickly killed the priest there.

Enheduanna had never felt surprised at what the commander said. She directly looked in Namtar s eyes:

"In this situation, you have to find your friend Pushu Ken otherwise you will be under danger."

The commander had just started to understand the importance of the case. He felt a sudden awe when he thought that the Holy Sister could suspect himself among others as well.

"With the order of Enheduanna, they took out the Elam man. The sculpturers started to compare the traces from the garden and the wall with the ones derived from the man. It was clear that both the traces, physically didn't look identical. The hand and the feet of Elam were smaller compared with the traces. He was not one of the murderers but it was clear that he had a connection with the murderers.

While the comparisons were made in the room, one of the soldiers came and said that they brought the corpse of the Priest Akiya and put on the ground in the hall. They all went to the hall taking the prints with them. The priest Akiya had been killed with a throat cut. His face was pale as his body lost all the blood. He couldn't have been killed so much before because his body was not so hard and was still warm. His murderer was certainly somewhere in the city because all the doors were locked. It was almost certain that Pushu Ken had killed him. He was one of the murderers if the Priest Akiya had been killed and it meant that the commander could be innocent but he could have any relation with the murder when thought that Pushu Ken was his friend. The Elam weapon trader? What was his position in this murder?

Elam trader was watching the corpse of the Priest Akiya on the chair sculpted from stone. Nakurtum had sensed the horror and nervousness in his glances that nobody else had realised. He was certainly in this murderer if he were the murderer or not. She whispered Enheduanna's ear about her worry. Enheduanna coming across Elam man:

"Do you know this man? she asked."

The man ignored the question. He was responding the questions in a silence mood. Commander Namtar interrupting:

"If the Holy Sister permits me, I know how to make him speak." he said.

When his words ended, the Elam man looked up at rising his head and spat at him instantly. The commander getting very angry, cleaning his face with the back of his hand fisted his jaw so hard that it fell off the chair. He started grunting pulling his knees back when he was hit his stomach after it. Things were out of control now. The commander daring as the Holy Sister didn't prevent him hit his head, too. Elam felt like faint and felt stupified. The commander shouted:

"Either you will speak right here or I will kill you here, you dirty creeper." he held his hair and sat him on the chair back.

Elam man hadn't felt his conscious yet. Meanwhile, the sculpturer said behind that the foot prints fit the Priest Akiya's prints exactly but the hand print didn't belong to him.

The Commander Namtar returned to the Elam man. He grabbed the right hand of the man, pushed the thumb and broke the finger. The sound his finger made had shaken both Enheduanna and Nakurtum. The man started screaming in pain. The shock he had felt brought him to his conscious. The commander grabbed his fourth finger.

"Won't you speak?" he asked.

When the man didn't respond, he broke it pushing it back hard. Then he grabbed the other finger. The Elam man was moaning in pain but was not speaking. The man could no longer bear the pain when his fingers were being broken one by one. He could pronounce only one word: "Lugal Ane!" and then he fainted.

It was a Sumerian name but didn't recall anything either to Enheduanna or Nakurtum. What was certain was that the causes of everything was the mysterious man so called Lugal Ane.

Enheduanna ordered that the corpse of the Priest Akiya must be buried to the city cemetery silently without any funerals. He would be buried without putting any signs and gifts representing the temple. The poem tablet which Enheduanna wrote about the damn of the Priest Akiya would be buried away with him so everybody would learn his deception to the Goddess Inanna wherever he went. Her orders were performed. He was thrown into a randomly dug cemetery like an animal rubbish and the tablet that Enheduanna had written was placed on his head side. The poem on the tablet was as followed:

Holy Inanna,
I am your order on the earth

Your Holy sister
This should be the end of all the deceivers,
Whoever he murdered,
must take their revenge
Sending him for your love Dumuzi
Damn on him on your sake forever
He must take his punishment under his order
I wrote all his sins in this pray

A perfect funeral had been made for the Priestess Amare in the evening. Her soul was sent away combining with the spiritual accompaniment of a large crowd in beautiful chants. She was buried in the special area in the rear temple reserved as the royal cemetery.

Enheduanna was sorry as the murderers hadn't been punished fully but she was full of love and hope for Amare. The pain of death was so real as the joy of love and they were both felt in the heart not in the body. She must heal her pains with her belief. The tears were the helplessness of the living people for that reason, she wouldn't cry. Today was a holy day. She had sacrificed her greatest gift to Inanna. Her temple was soaked by the blood of a priestess sacrificing her life for her. There was no greater present than this. Why should she feel sorry on such day? The beautiful Amare had earned her love. She had reached Inanna that she had sacrificed her life for. Maybe today wasn't holy birthday but it must have been the holy death day. Today must have been a great wedding as a present for the friend but a bullet for the enemy.

She ordered Nakurtum to inform the people that this evening would be held as a holy funeral and entertainment day, the whole temple must get ready and products would be delivered for the soul of Amare and forgiveness of Inanna. But she had only one condition:

"Those who want to make offer to the Goddess must present only roses, nothing else.

Nakurtum, ordering the three priests that they must announce to the people in the city about the funeral of Amare left the temple. The sun was about to set. The west side of the city was in full crimson and the south side was in full darkness. The stars had started to appear slowly and shed small lights over the night. The bird songs had been replaced by grasshopper sounds. The servicers would start turning on the street lights soon. There was nobody but the few people returning to their homes from the works. Nakurtum walking on thinking of the things she had gone through on the day couldn't understand how fast she came to the military quarter. She found herself at the door of the station, in front of the guard soldier.

Good evening soldier, I want to see the lieutenant Eluti. she said. The soldier went into the quarter telling her to wait there and returned with the Lieutenant Eluti after a short time.

"The Priestess Nakurtum, I hope nothing else worse had happened." he said.

No, my lieutenant, thank God, it didn't. But we need to speak."

"Of course, please come in."

When Nakurtum heard his invitation, she hesitated

for a moment. Entering inside had both startled her and she didn't want others to hear her. In a soft tone:

"Let's speak outside the lieutenant if possible."

The lieutenant, accepting her offer put his arms in her and helped her to the harbour where the boats and sandals were tied. They sat on the stone chairs made for the fishermen without realising that two eyes watching them. Nakurtum started speaking shyly looking into his eyes.

"My lieutenant, I need your help, it is both urgent and very important."

"Of course, my priestess, if it is something I could do. What is the problem?"

Nakurtum told him the things that he didn't know happening in the temple. She told him that the statue pieces loaded in the cars must be taken away as soon as possible. The lieutenant firstly startled and then surprised of what he had heard. He stood and paced a few steps. He started scratching his hair. Looking at her:

"Who can dare such a thing, also on the celebration day and among so many people?" he expressed his calmness.

"That day must be chosen consciously, lieutenant, because nothing done in the hall could be heard due to the noise of the music and drums in the garden. And of course, the crowd would make the discovery of the murderers harder."

"Then, who else can know the secret things you spoke with the princess? Whoever knew it had done what you must do before you. I wish, they had cleared the pieces of the statues they had broken." he said smiling.

"I have no idea, Amare must have blurted out to someone else."

Nakurtum had bent her head first, her eyes filled with the tears. Saying Amare's name reminded her of death. She stood up cleaning her cheeks and eyes using her hands. She went towards the lieutenant and held his hands with her wet hands. They caught each others eyes.

"I request one more thing from you, lieutenant."

The lieutenant holding her hands in his, lifted them to his lips and kissed softly.

"Of course, my priestess, I am at your service."

She had felt shy of his last behaviour. For the first time, a man had kissed her hands. Her face blushed. She felt embarrassed. She bent her head. She pulled her hands back as if to hide them.

"The Commander Namtar had his old uniform that he had taken off on the celebration day under his bed, I want you to check it to see if it had blood traces, if it had, I want you to bring it to me. Please, don't forget to fetch his reed pencil on the table."

"Never tell me that you suspect the commander. I think he is the last person to commit such a crime."

"Not my Holy Sister but I have been suspecting him since the beginning of the murder. The most deceptive enemy is the one you never think him/her to be, isn't it, lieutenant.?

Without speaking more, she left him saying: "Hope to see you in the holy funeral to be held for the Priestess Amare in the evening." She started walking towards the temple in the shaking and gloomy lights of the streets. The darkness had fully absorbed the city Ur.

The streets illuminated by the lights of the one, two and three floored bricked houses were finer to walk on these times. She was watching the shadow games while she was walking carefully, her head bent down, and checking her left and right sides from time to time. When she was about to reach the city centre, she felt a shadow was following her. She quickened her steps and looked back, she saw that the shadow disappeared among the houses. When she was turning first street after walking for more, she instantly looked at the right, then she made sure that the shadow was coming after her because it had disappeared among the houses again. Someone was following her and it was closing her in every step. She had a long distance to reach the temple. Running wouldn't do any good, either. After thinking for a while, she threw herself in an empty area between two houses. Here was pitch black. She leaned on one of the wall crouching. She fixed her eyes on the road and started waiting silently. Her breathings eased. She felt a sudden awe due to death. She could hear the beatings of her heart. She covered her face completely and started watching through her fingers. She could hear that foot steps were closing in. It was not so hard for her to understand that the shadow was stopping due to the stopping foot steps. The steps started again. It came closer and closer& The sounds stopped again when it came across her. The shadow following her

154

was just in front of her. The man had stopped and was looking around himself, possibly trying to hear the foot steps he thought to belong to Nakurtum. The shadow of the sword in his hand reflected on the ground. Then he heard different foot steps on the right. As the noise was complicated, it showed that the comers were more than one. The man following her must have heard the same sounds and ran away towards where he had come wearing his swords. She saw that three soldiers appeared in front of the area she hid herself. She came out:

"Help, help, please save me!" she asked for help in his broken and frightened voice.

She could hardly speak when the soldier hearing her voice reached her:

"A man, an armed man was following me. He ran away towards there before you came. she could say.

The soldiers had understood from the dress of Nakurtum that she was a high priestess closer to the temple. The cloth of the dress she was wearing was both qualified and special. The stones of the rings on her fingers and the bracelet on her wrist were very precious. They were not something that every priestesses could wear. The soldier responsible for the patrol pointed her to calm down.

"Please calm down, priestess, I will do what is necessary." ordering his soldiers to fetch the man going to the area Nakurtum had shown.

The soldier jumped to do what they were ordered. The authorised soldier staying there stared at her from head to toe.

"What are you doing in the streets at this time, don't you know that only badness accompanies to the person walking through the darkness alone at these times."

Nakurtum responded in a calm tone to the soldier who was taller and wider shouldered without seeing his face:

"I had a meeting with the quarter lieutenant. It had just finished and I was returning to the temple. There is a funeral in the temple in a few hours and I must catch up with it."

"If you want, I can accompany you, the danger could re-appear."

She had felt happy for this offer. The last thing she would want at that time was to stay alone in the gloomy street light hardly illuminating the street.

Expressing her pleasure, she walked together with the soldier in strides without speaking.

When they reached the temple, the priests and the priestesses were hurriedly working to prepare the great garden for the evening. The Inanna statue in the altar hall had been placed near the platforms on which she and enheduanna would sit. What else attracting her attention was that four soldiers had been ordered on the each side of the garden. She walked through the whole garden after thanking and sending the soldier accompanying her through the temple door. She checked the preparations. Then she headed towards the kitchen area. She turned there when she saw that sand had been piled on the empty area on the right. When she approached the pile, she saw a deep well filled with woods that she couldn't understand why. She turned back and did her checks in an order. She looked for Enheduanna but she wasn't around. She went to her room thinking that she could be there. She had doubt about telling her what's happened before coming or not. She didn't want to worry the Holy Sister more. When she made up her mind not to tell, she had reached the door of her room. She knocked at the door softly and entered the room. She found her getting ready for the funeral. She had worn her black clothes whose skirt was decorated with gold leaves and wore her black scarf on her head. She was tinging black kohl. She greeted her hands in the front.

"Welcome the priestess, is everything alright, it took a long time to come back."

Nakurtum started feeling the same pessimism that she had while coming. Enheduanna continued speaking while Nakurtum was still doubtful to tell her or not.

"I asked the commander to order a soldier on each corner to prevent the same things from happening again. Isn't it wise, is it? What do you think?"

To skip that question, Nakurtum chose to answer without thinking:

"Whatever you order is right, my Holy Sister but something had attracted my attention. The well full of wood on the bank of the garden?"

"Surprise, dear priestess, it will be the surprise of the night." she said smiling.

Showing the perfume bottles on the right side of the table:

"Which of them must we wear this evening, you choose and let's wear the same this time."

Nakurtum got the charming and distorting perfume giving the best smell to Enheduanna's skin which was the mixture of hyacinth and jasmine seeds. She took a drop on her finger and put it against Enheduanna's neck, wrists, upper breasts and arm pits. Then she put her crown decorated with the jewelries looking like golden leaves and daisy flowers, representing Inanna on her scarf covering her woven and piled hair. She cleaned her sandals standing near her bed and help her wear them. Enheduanna was ready now.

Nakurtum wanted permission to go to her room to get ready but:

"No need, the priestess, come and get which dress you want out of the box. Please hurry up, we have lots of things to do yet." she responded.

She took out and wore the brown, decorated dress that she saw on Enheduanna , worn from backward to front, whose edges were hand made. She sat on her chair and let her prepare Nakurtum. Enheduanna carefully tinged her the same kohl and sprayed the same perfume. She combed her hair and helped her wear the scarf. They were both ready for the funeral from now on.

When Nakurtum looked through the window, she saw that people started gathering. The musicians had taken their places and were waiting for Enheduanna's orders. People had already sat at the tables in groups and was waiting for the hot and fresh breads to be delivered.

When she looked at the entrance door of the temple, he saw that the Lieutenant Eluti was sitting on a chair and watching the garden. He didn't have his military uniform on him. She realised that he looked more handsome in his casual clothes. She turned to Enheduanna:

"My Holy Sister, the people had gathered up and took their places. We can go down to the garden if you are ready." said she.

After Enheduanna confirmed, they put their arms in each others and got down to the garden to take their places in the funeral.

159

The celebrations started after the sun set and the stars shone in the sky. The perfect and various flowers gathered from Ur mountains, valleys and river banks had been presented to the Inanna Statue placed in the garden as an offer. Prays and wishes were made. The best chants from the tablets Enheduanna had written was sung out.

Enheduanna, standing up, raising her hands started speaking loudly. Everybody focused on her:

My public! I am the Holy Sister of the Queen of the heaven Inanna making our country fertile; the Goddess of the moon shedding light over the darkness, gifting victories, the owner of the earth and the sky. It shall be known from now on that this temple belongs solely to Inanna. You will make all your prays and offers to the only Goddess of this country Inanna. Know that the other Gods you have adorn are like the flies hovering over the blood of the animals you have offered. You are still free to adorn which God you want but you can only present your prays and offers only to Inanna in this temple. Inanna promises you abundance and fertility. She drops rain on your farms in every autumn and winter. She promises babies for your animals and children for your homes. She only demands you to adorn her. This is her wish from you. Like the people getting on the ship of Utnapiş-tim found the salvation so be the ones sheltering in my temple. Those who aren't pleased with her should leave our city at once before being damned or live in the heaven in this country till they die.

After she finished her words, a deep silence broke out. People froze in shock as they didn't know what to say or do looking at each other. It didn't last much. A man in the middle of the crowd stood up, raised his hands and started speaking loud:

Holy Inanna, Holy Inanna!

The people hearing his scream started to stand up in different numbers of groups and raised their hands accompanying him:

The Holy Inanna, Holy Inanna,

Enheduanna raised her hands palms facing up accompanied them for a few minutes. Then she pointed them to stop and sit down. She continued speaking:

Believing only in Inanna is to be abundant, fertility, health, animals with many babies and peaceful homes with children. The price of deception to Inanna is death. There are deceiving people among us. There are people making bad plans for Enheduanna

-the Holy Sister of Inanna. I will present one of them to you a little later. You will punish it, not me.

Everybody cheered her up, clapped hands and confirmed her.

Commander, bring the guilty to me.

The commander and the two soldiers waiting at the altar door approached the platform where Enheduanna stood with the Elam weapon trader with them. Enheduanna showing the Elam man:

"That is one of them, One of the murderers killing the Priestess Amare who was the assistant of the Holy Sister being the priestess of Inanna. Dear Amare found her peace with Inanna and it is time to help him face the anger of Inanna. Tell me, what kind of punishment he deserves?

Thousands of people in the garden started shouting after Enheduanna:

Death, death, death!

Enheduanna, letting the crowd shout for a time pointed to stop. Then she got the firebrand hanged on the wall of the temple and handed it to Nakurtum.

"Then, Commander Namtar, his punishment is death, start the fire."

When the commander approached Enheduanna and got the firebrand, the Elam weapon trader started speaking and begging:

"I am innocent, I didn't do anything, Pushu Ken did everything, I am not guilty."

Enheduanna, turning to Elam man:

"What the hell were you doing in my city, then?"

He was shaking and crying violently due to the fear. He hardly answered among his chokes:

"I only brought the weapons Pushu Ken had demanded."

This answer was more horrifying than Enheduanna had expected.

"Where are the weapons now then?"

"I don't know, I submitted them all to him and got my money, that's all."

The public started shouting again after they had heard the conversation between the Elam man and Enheduanna. The commander had already set the wood in the well on the bank of the garden in fire. The flames were rising so high that it was like the height of a man out of the well. Enheduanna turned her head towards the people in the garden and let her eyes stay on them for a time. "Set him on fire, Inanna's punishment was the hot flames rising up the sky. The punishment of a crime in my country is to die burning." she shouted.

The soldier held the man's arm begging for forgiveness and trying to save himself and brought to the bank of the well. All the people in the garden had turned towards the well and watching what was going on. Some had fears on their faces and some had joys. When Enheduanna pointed, the commander hit the Elam man hard on his face and threw him to the fire. Painful cries had been heard for a time and then his voice was swept away. His body had been purified by fire from his deception and he had burned to death. Enheduanna turned to the people and spoke loudly:

"This evening is the celebration of Amare and her love Inanna coming together. My beautiful Amare, your destination be the heaven garden. Upon you be the love and blessings of Inanna, your soul be at peace." ended her speech.

She turned to the musicians and gestured them to start. When the priestess started mastering on their devices, the fear and nervousness left away. People felt more relaxed when the beers and breads were delivered on the tables.

People started tasting the beers when the best songs of Mesopotamia were being sung. Enheduanna was joining the celebration with Commander and her solely assistant Nakurtum on her sides, dancing with the people among them and singing with the singers going closer to them. She came to her table from time to time and sipped her beer. Nakurtum seeing that the Holy Sister sat at her table, taking this chance,

"My Holy Sister, only owner of my skin and soul, the queen of Inanna on the earth, May I request something from you?" she said.

She pulled her head back and continued watching the dancers.

Enheduanna responded the same:

"Your desire be my wish, my priestess, tell me what it is?"

"I had promised something to the Priestess Urnina whom I had mentioned you. I need an assistant and comrade while doing your orders enthusiastically. I would like you to let her with me and assign her as my assistant, my Holy Sister."

"How much you trust in her, my priestess?"

"She dared helping me even at the hardest time of mine, she never scared of the damn of the Gods and showed her faith to Inanna. I trust her as much as I trust myself, my Holy Sister."

"What a person could achieve the highest is the trust of someone, my beautiful priestess. She had already achieved that degree earning your trust, do however you want. Go and call her to our table. In addition to this, I will assign the young Priest Abram on the behalf of the deceiver Priest Akiya."

The Priestess jump on her feet feeling utmost happy, found the Priestess Urnina and told her about the situation. Urnina screamed in a joy. She hugged Nakurtum. They came to the table of Enheduanna together. They greeted her and sat. Enheduanna filled in the cup from the pitcher. She handed it to the Priestess Urnina looking into her shining eyes joyfully. Urnina got the cup in her shaking hand. She turned to Enheduanna standing up.

"Drinking for your holy personality, beauty and devotion, my dear princess. I am really thankful to you." She drank the whole glass at one sip and sat back out of breath.

The Priestess Nakurtum hugged her with her right left arm and made a kiss on her cheek. Then she took permission from Enheduanna whispering something into her ear and went to the lieutenant Eluti. He was sitting near the main entrance of the temple and drinking his beer. He had a friend with him. He stood up and greeted nodding gently when he saw that she was coming towards him.

"Good evening, lieutenant, I am glad you had come."

"That pleasure belong to me, priestess, it is great to see you again."

Nakurtum smiled softly.

"If you want, let's get to work at once instead of wasting time. I'll show you the cars. Let s finish this work as soon as possible."

166   The lieutenant nodded and they went to the area in which the cars full of the statue pieces were parked.

Firstly, he checked the things under the blankets, and then covered the pieces back carefully to prevent them from being seen.

"Never worry, my Priestess, you can be sure that all these had been removed and buried under the deserted thin sand of the desert after the ceremony. Meanwhile, here is the pen of Namtar. I got it off his table."

He handed the pen wrapped up in a cloth to Nakurtum and continued:

"For the clothes, they were still under the bed and didn't have any trace of blood, priestess," he said.

"Be sure that you will be rewarded for your help, lieutenant. thank you very much."

"The greatest reward to me would be to see you again, my priestess."

Nakurtum greeted him bending her head and returned to the platform at which Enheduanna was sitting. She sat on her place and opened the cloth covering the pen. After checking the pen carefully poked Enheduanna to draw her attention to the matter. Enheduanna asked whispering, Isn't this the pen of the one I had predicted?

Nakurtum nodded in confirmation. While Enheduanna and the commander were raising their glasses for love and peace, they were chatting at the same time. The commander was still wondering if Enheduanna still thought he was one of the suspects but he was not eager to ask this directly. It caused a great annoyance for him. As Pushu Ken hadn't been caught yet, it was increasing the suspects on him, because he was his friend and staying with him as his guest. No matter how nervous he was, he couldn't take his eyes from Enheduanna. While he was looking at smooth, goddess beauty of her face in admiration and love, he was going on drinking his beer without any stop. After each glass, the amount of alcohol in his veins are getting more, he was feeling that his conscious were getting more foggy despite feeling more at ease. This was what he wanted. While the entertainment continued, Enheduanna whispered into his ear:

"All the glasses having been raised so far are for Amare and Inanna, dear commander but I wish to raise for me from now on."

The Commander Namtar tried to speak fluently but his half drunk tongue responded in a sorrowful tone:

"All the raising glasses of my country must be for your honor, my Holy Sister."

"As far as I see, the wine has made you quite gentle, commander."

"Not at all, it is your own gentleness, my Holy Sister. The real thing making me so gentle is your perfect and unresistable beauty."

Enheduanna tried to keep herself but couldn't help sending out a loud laughter. Even Nakurtum and Urnina had heard this laughter. While they were looking into her eyes curiously, she blinked to Nakurtum. this meant Don't worry, everything is ok.

168   When Enheduanna asked him about his military adventures, the stories of the heroships he had had, he started telling the stories boasting like every soldier. Meanwhile, Enheduanna was filling the empty glasses any more. The ceremony was about to end. The public started to get the delivered products and set out for their homes but his adventurous stories were not coming to an end.

"Commander, your stories are really interesting, how about telling the rest in my room?" she asked.

This was what the commander had hoped for years but couldn't hear it by that time. He couldn't miss such a chance. With the best princess of Mesopotamia, with the Holy Sister of the Goddess Inanna and also in her room? He nodded his head showing that he accepted the offer eagerly.

Enheduanna ordered her assistants Nakurtum and Urnina to help the commander to go to her room and said that she would come after them. The priestesses did what they were ordered. They helped the commander taking his arms and helped him go up to her room. Enheduanna went to the study room first and then walked to the rest room getting a pitcher of wine and two glasses. When she reached the corridor turning to her room, she met Nakurtum and Urnina. She wanted them to pay attention that the work downstairs must be completed and the temple doors be closed properly.

While Nakurtum and Urnina walked on the long and gloomy corridors, they started talking about the Priestess Urnina to replace Amare. Although Nakurtum and Urnina were very close friends, work mates, secret sharers, one side of the room they all had shared was empty from now on. Whenever they came to the room, seeing that empty side and feeling sorry wouldn't do any good. If life had given the people what it had gotten from them, the fortune wouldn't have exposed the people to death. Sharing her loneliness in Amare's absence would force her to go deeper in a more painful loneliness.Her tears which would start dropping whenever she remembered her would grow her memories but they wouldn't bring her back to life.

The best thing to be done is to move Urnina where she must be as soon as possible. The Priestess Urnina would go down to the floor where seclusion rooms were situated, would pick up her belongings and come up to the room where she would share with Nakurtum. Meanwhile, Nakurtum would gather up Amare's belongings and bed and make the room ready for her till she came. That was the plan.

When Nakurtum came to the room, she changed her clothes first. Then she opened the wooden box in which Amare placed her clothes and started to put them near the wall one by one. The first dress was her night gown that she had taken off last and put in her box. She stared at it for a time and smelled it. Her sweat had been on the dress and smelled like amare. She closed her eyes and felt as if Amare was with her. She couldn't help her tears and her eyes felt foggy. She smelled again and put down on the ground as it had been folded. She took out all the carefully folded dresses one by one and piled up near the box. She got the sack made of thick cloth in which she put her nail clipper, needle and rope, ear sticks, rings and her brooches that she had stuck to her clothes. She put the sack on the ground to prevent the contents falling down and opened the sack slowly. She thought that she could save the brooches as a memory. She put the jewelries made of precious stones and different colours on the left. While she was about to close the sack, she realised there was another wrap in the middle of the sack. She opened it wondering what it could hold. She saw plant leaves and something like dried fruit pieces that she couldn't make any meanings of. When she was fingering through the leaves, the Priestess Urnina entered the room. She left the dresses in her arms on the sofa Amare had been sleeping and crouched near Nakurtum. When she saw that Nakurtum was looking at something carefully,

"Is there any problem, the priestess? you are very pensive." she asked.

She handed out the wrap to Urnina with its contents.

"I found it in Amare's belongings but I couldn't get what it was. I had never seen this among her belongings."

Urnina got the wrap and looked at the dry fruit pieces and the leaves in it.

"I think, I know what they are, my priestess. I had served for the oil healer before becoming seclusion responsible. I saw such leaves at that time."

"What is the use of these leaves, was Amare ill?"

"No, my priestess, it is poisonous plant. It is called deadly nightshade. Even one leaf of it is enough to kill a person."

Nakurtum felt surprised. While she was thinking what Amare could do with these plants:

"For the sake of Inanna, She..." she stammered.

"She," what? the priestess.

Nakurtum fell in a deep and frightening silence closing her face with her hands. After thinking for a time, she responded Urnina's question.

"I have understood why the Priestess Amare had been killed."

She folded the wrap carefully and stood up. She took her night gown off and wore one of her clean dress.

"We need to speak the Holy Sister at once."

The Priestess Urnina asked her unable to understand why Nakurtum behaved like that:

"At this time of the night? she has a guest, she can get angry with us."

"I am sure she isn't asleep. Come on, we are going. I am sure you'll understand everything there."

They went out of the room together and started walking toward Enheduanna s room.

When Enheduanna entered the room after talking to the priestesses, the commander had taken off his clothes, sat on the bed leaning back on the wall and was drinking wine from the pitcher remaining from yesterday. His muscled body and his calves were fully visible and attractive. His half whitened chest and groin hair showed his maturity. The way his hand shook while raising his glass to his mouth showed that he had drunk enough.

Enheduanna left the things in hands under the table and sat near him. She started caressing the hair on his chest using her right hand. He started feeling above the clouds with her soft touches and loosing his conscious under the effect of the beer. While he leaned forward to kiss Enheduanna, she pulled her head aside and prevented him. When the commander leaned back on the wall again, she caressed downward in an attractive and soft touch.

"Dear Namtar, I wonder my commander honors his Holy Sister a cup of wine as being a gentle soldier?" she asked.

The Commander Namtar tried to sit back and responded in a dizzy tone like his head:

"Your wish is my order but you will be my Holy Whore instead of my Holy Sister."

He hardly stood up and went to the table shaking and hardly walking. He got the pitcher and tried to fill in the cup with beer. Half of the wine was pouring in the cup and the other half was on the ground. Enheduanna seeing his odd behaviours went to the table smiling in her heart and got the pitcher out of his hand.

"If you continue trying to pour like, I think we won't have any beer to drink, commander, let me fill in."

While she was pouring both her cup and the commander's cup, he returned to the bed shaking and hardly walking like he did before. Enheduanna, giving the beer in her right hand to the commander raised her other hand:

"Let's drink for the soul of my beautiful amare and her owner Inanna." she said.

They finished their cups at one sip. When she returned after filling their glasses once more, the commander had already been in a deep sleep. Enheduanna smiled. She sat on the sofa near the window and started watching his naked body drinking her beer. When she stood up to fill in her cup, she heard the door knock softly and opened it before the second knock.

In front of her was Nakurtum with a wrap in her hand and Urnina. She looked back at the commander who was still asleep in the bed. She went out as she saw that he was not awake. She closed the door behind.

"Is there a problem at this time of the night, Nakurtum?"

"My Holy Sister, you must see this." she said handing out the wrap in her hand.

She unwrapped the sack carefully and when she saw the contents:

"What are these?" she asked in a surprise.

"While I was gathering up the belongings of Amare before Urnina moved to my room, I found this in her box, my lady." Then she looked at Urnina as if to say that she must go ahead.

"My Holy Sister, I had worked with the Healer before, I saw these leaves there. They are called deadly night shade and it is very poisonous. Even a leaf could be enough to kill a person.

Enheduanna fell into thoughts looking both at Urnina and the wrap in her hand.

"It can't be, I never want to believe" she said and crouched down.

Nakurtum crouched near her and put her hand on her shoulder. In a tone that she could hear:

"I think I have discovered the meaning of the message sent to Amare: "don't cook the food.""

Enheduanna was shocked by what she had learned. The words came across her pale lips:

"I could guess, the priestess."

She was both angry and sorry. She sat where she had been for a time and she stood up.

"Come to the room with me, Nakurtum. Priest Urnina, you wait here, too."

They went to the room together. Nakurtum left the wrap containing the poisonous plants on the table. Then, she took out the sack containing the foot and hand prints that she had brought from her room. First, she got the foot print and then the shoe of the commander near the bed and came to the table. They checked if the two were compatible with each other. It was impossible! The prints were not compatible with each other. Enheduanna got the hand print at once and they went to the bed. Nakurtum grabbed his hand softly and placed it on to the hand print. The hand prints weren't compatible, either because the commander was wearing his agate stone silver ring on his left hand but on the print, the ring was on this left hand. Both Enheduanna and Nakurtum had failed in their predictions. They were so sure that one of the murderers was the commander that they both felt disappointed. Enheduanna went out holding Nakurtum's hand. They went to her room to be able to assess the matter cooly.

The sun started to rise and its lights were shining on the commander's face with all their warmth. He tried to get away from the lights turning his face for a few times but he couldn't get rid of the lights, he tried to cover his face with his hands. He couldn't move his hands. He wanted to sit up opening his eyes but he couldn't, either. When he looked down, he saw that his hands and feet were tied to the sofa he was lying on. Then he saw Enheduanna sitting on a chair in front of him and the priestess Nakurtum and Urnina watching crouching near him. While he still bore the drunkness remaining from yesterday and the drowsiness, he started speaking in a shocked and pesimist mood:

"What is going on here, why have you tied me?"

Due to the excessive alcohol he had taken, his mouth and throat had been dry and he felt very thirsty. He coughed softly a few times. Nakurtum got the pitcher on the table and helped him drink a few sips of wine to ease his thirst and sat back.

"I know everything, the commander. I am waiting for you to speak."

The commander hardly collected the words as if stupified by being beaten so much:

"What have you realised, the Holy Sister, what do you mean?" he could manage to ask.

"Don't pretend not to understand, commander, don't force me."

"I couldn't get anything from your words, please untie me otherwise, you must bear the consequences."

"You have killed the Priestess Amare."

"Nonsense, the Holy Sister, I don't have anything to do with the things having happened."

"Firstly, you had persuaded the Priestess Amare to poison me or you had believed to persuade her. But the Priestess Amare didn't do anything like that and didn't want to do it, either. You were afraid that she would inform me when she didn't poison me. You had looked for opportunities to prevent her from speaking to me. You had called her behind the temple on the offer day. You got into the action via the nose and the crowd. When she didn't die after the Priest Akiya knifed through her heart, you cut her throat to end her life using your sword before she started screaming. When Nakurtum realised you, you escaped, wore your uniform and returned to the temple to join the entertainment. You sat near me."

The commander responded with a loud laughter to the things he heard. He demanded Nakurtum to give him wine for his drying lips and mouth.

The Priest did what he wanted. She helped him drink the wine.

Enheduanna decided to go over him once more to be able to learn something else from him.

"I don't expect you to confess the commender because I am sure that you are one of the murderers. While you were sleeping, I matched the foot and hand prints with your own hands and foot. Both of them were compatible with yours. It is very strange that you are the other murderer of Amare."

"You are a very beautiful and emotional woman. YOu have a very kind heart, perfect poems and prays but you can't think logically, the priestess Enheduanna. Please stop bluffing, I haven't kill the Priestess Amare. You know it, too. If the prints were compatible with mine, it is totally coincidence."

He had fixed his eyes on the Holy Sister's eyes in hatred and anger. He was trying to choke. Before he wanted, Nakurtum helped him drink one cup of wine.

"Please, untie me, I can help you."

He took a few deep breathes. He watched the bluish color of the sky and the seeds on the newly rising branches of the tree in the terrace.

"I can help you because I have things that I know, my princess."

Enheduanna surprised and curious:

"I wonder what you could know more than I do." she said smiling.

"I will tell you what I know but I have a condition."

The commander bent his head down. He felt the depression of being caught instead of regret. He had prepared everything and stayed silent for the murder of the two persons. He continued his speech being eager to have his punishment in a sorrowful attitude.

"Promise me that you would forgive me and wouldn't punish me after I have told you the whole story."

"It completely depends on what I would hear from you, the commander. Tell me the truth and earn your freedom back."

The commander smiled at what he had heard.

"The realities are the matter of perception. Things had happened but not finished yet. I can't change the realities but can help you prevent the things to happen in the future. I can show your honor to the public."

Enheduanna was confused by the previous sentence that the commander told. "Things happened but not finished yet." What could it mean? It was both a clear threat and a warning. She felt that there were different things in Amare's murder. The weapons Elam man had brought were not in vain, of course. It was clear that the answers of all these questions were hidden in the commander.

"It is not important if my public sees my honor, but my enemies must see it. Speak ahead, commander, I am listening to you. I promise on the behalf of Inanna, I would not punish you for your confessions."

"The only guilt of mine for you was to let them enter weapons and men into the city."

She thought that the matter was more serious than she had thought. Weapons and men showed that a direct plan had been made for her and the city.

"For whom and why did you do this, commander?"

"For Lugal Ane, my princess."

He started coughing as if to tear his lungs. He wanted to sit up softly to be able to breathe better but it was impossible. His hands were tied. He looked at Nakurtum begging while coughing. She waited for Enheduanna's permission to give him some more wine. When the Holy Sister nodded towards the water pitcher, Nakurtum filled in the glass and served the commander. The commander cleaned his throat.

"You know my princess, little time left for my retirement. I can only meet my expenses of drinks with the retirement amount your father would give. The man offered silver of my ten years retirement salary via my friend Pushu Ken and I didn't have any other choice but to accept."

Enheduanna narrowed her eyes, frowned and shouted at the commander angrily:

"Damn it commander, have you deceived me and my father-the great king Sargon just for silver?"

The commander turning his eyes to the window tried to escape her glance. when he heard the damn sound of the crow on the side of the window, he thought that it was the sign of a bad luck. He started to have neck-ache as he had to speak rising his head all the time. Enheduanna continued speaking:

"Damn it, commander! Not me but you abused my father's trust in you. Who is this Lugal Ane? What does he want?"

"I have no idea who he is but what I know is that he wants the throne you are sitting at now so he wants to own both the city and the temple."

"Why did they kill Amare? And the broken statues?"

"She would have been the Holy Sister of temple and he would have married her on the Holy Day. They persuaded Amare promising this and wanted her to poison you but Amare didn't do this. I think she regretted later. They had to kill her before she told you the whole story. They did it, too.

Things were falling into place slowly. The secret sentences on the tablet found in Amare's pocket had found their true meaning. Amare had either regretted or couldn't find time to cook the food which meant to poison Enheduanna in other words and via the commander, "the flocks had entered the barn." The weapons had been brought to the city and hidden somewhere."

"And the statue of Gods, why did they need to break them before I moved them to somewhere else?"

The commander was getting worse, the pain in his stomach was increasing, his throat was drying more and the pain in his chest was getting worse, too.

He felt that he had less power to speak and he was feeling more sweat each moment. He wished to end this torture and leave this place as soon as possible. To the farthest place riding on his horse.

"They would have provoked the public against you after breaking the statues at that night. People in the entertainment would get annoyed when they saw that the statues of the Gods they adorned and prayed had been broken. They would have possibly crushed you. Don't forget that everybody was drunk at that night and doing this was very easy."

He looked at Nakurtum and smiled:

"When the Priestess Nakurtum acted before them and collected the broken pieces, their plan was spoiled."

The commander was getting more sweat every minute and his pain was unbearable now. He didn't have enough power to lift his head to speak any more. He could say from the sofa in a low voice:

"I don't feel well, the Holy Sister,"

Enheduanna approached the commander so closely and looked into his eyes feeling mercy for him.

"You are too late to tell the truth, commander, too late. Before I promised you, you drank the poisoned wine that you wanted Amare to kill me with. I can't do anything for you. What you were afraid of while you were living, it must be your punishment after death."

His body strained so much. He started shaking in periods.

He was grunting among his breathings like a man whose lungs were full of water. The sounds coming out of his lips became more horrifying each minute. He was straining as if to vomit. A minute later, he exhaled his last breath staring at the side wall in empty glances and foams coming out of his mouth.

A deep silence has prevailed in the room and everybody was staring at the lifeless and naked body of the commander in deep thoughts. The door knocked violently. It was opened when the knocking person was allowed to enter. the Lieutenant Eluti was in front of them. He started speaking in fearful, shaking, quick and nervous tone: His eyes were watching the lifeless, naked, lying and tied body of the commander.

"My Holy Sister, something very, very urgent case is happening. The public is gathering in the centre and the crowd is increasing each minute. I think it is the preparation for a rebellion, my lady."

Enheduanna, unable to believe what she had heard stood up at once. She went towards the door. She hadn't predicted that things could start so quickly. While she had just learned the truth, the things having happened now were too early and unexpected. Watching the trees in the terrace and the people doing their daily routines out of the temple,

"Lieutenant, go to the police station, gather the soldiers and bring them in front of the temple. Nakurtum, get out all the children and priestesses of the temple, get the soldiers in and lock the doors. Urnina, gather all the priests in the small garden. Open the weapon depot and give weapon to all of them.. she said ordering each servant."

The lieutenant waiting for Enheduanna finish her words could speak in a sad, hesitant and hardly speaking tone: "My Princess, the soldiers are among the rebellions, too."

While Enheduanna was waiting for the rewards as she carried out of the wish of the Goddess Inanna, what happened was too far. She never expected that things could go such worse.

She had to fight in addition to doing what is necessary for her belief. Maybe, the Gods got angry and demanded blood But the blood sacrificed could be an offer for Inanna not for the other Gods. When this war ended, all the Gods would kneel down and express their obediences to Inanna.

Who is Enheduanna?

Enheduanna is the first writer and the poet of the world lived 2.300 B.C. Some information was revealed on the tablets discovered during the excavations in the city Ur carried out the Archaeologist Leonard Wooleyin 1925. There is not much information about her. She is known to be the daughter of Akad King Sargon i, and was assigned as a Holy Sister for the most important temple in Ur by her father.

The majority of her poems were written about the Goddess Inanna. The meaning of her name is "The Holy Sister of the proud of the heaven." Her real name is not known.

The poems and prays had been read out in the temples for about 500 years after her death. The academist and researcher Paul Kriwaczek writes these about her: "Her compositions, despite being re-discovered in our era had continued surviving as wish words for centuries. Via the Babylonians, they had affected the Bible written in Hebrew and inspired the chants and prays of Greek Homeros. Even the clergies of the early Christian church had seen the ongoing reflections of Enheduanna who was known as the first literature writer throughout the history.

Her effect lasting throughout her life was so important as her literature heritage. Enheduanna not only had gone beyond the heavy responsibilities given by her father but also affected the whole culture of her period. Via her written works, she changed the concept of the nature of Mesopotamia Gods and humans were divine.

In addition to these works being aesthetic and beautiful, it had a great impact of Mesopotamia theology. To make a richer art concept, she made the Gods more understandable by the public synthesizing Sumerians and Akad believes. For instance, her thoughts about the God of the moon Inanna to make Inanna a more sympathetic and deeper character and she raised as the queen of the heaven instead of a local Goddess. She transformed these two names via her works and they looked more merciful than before. They became as Gods or Goddesses not only for Sumerians or Akads but also for all the people in the region.

The scientists have discovered that the old Babylon texts in the archives of Nippur were the original chant copies of Neo Sumers. These chants had a great impact on religious heritage. It had a clear and important social role from the Delfi Temple oracles in Greece to the dancer priestesses, warrior priestesses and Amazons.

Enheduanna sang songs containing praise and offer to the Goddess and used an instrument like lyre, possibly invented by chance in Ur. She was serving as an assistant for her father who was very passionate to extent his colonist empire from Asia to the near east.

The political and religious realities that she looked into in her chants had given her the fame of a poet and a prophet. The first narration of enheduanna known as the first literature writer in world history, started as follows: "I am Enheduanna!" This was a great attempt in history. Thousands of poems, prays or songs remained as mystery till that day became non anonymous works and whose writers and composers were known to the people after enheduanna.

In the temple, women were educated and important writers were grown up, as well. As literacy was limited by only a powerful elite group, writing and creating art belonged only to higher class.

Inanna was Enheduanna's literary work with her poetic compositions, temple chants collections and the divine chants devoted only for the Goddess Inanna. In antique Sumerians, a woman could only get her place on the top of the literature when she had become a princess. She was first woman poet registered in history. She took her place among the other important leaders due to her role in combining the two different sides in cult worship in Sumer and akad, using language and different traditions.

In the middle east geography absorbed by the Gods and male dominance on the whole life, Enheduanna was the first heroine of the women, a Holy Sister sanctifying the empire of her father king i Sargon declaring himself as the king and a great bureaucrat earning the respect of her people. The remainings of her stories that she presented to us thousands of years ago still affect the many areas of the popular culture in our era.*

The current ruin of the Temple of Ur

Sumerian gods

Inanna

REHBER KİTAP

Yazar Adayının Yolculuğu

"Tüm muhteşem hikayeler iki şekilde başlar;ya
bir insan bir yolculuğa çıkar,ya da şehre bir
yabancı gelir..."
TOLSTOY

ALI ERYILMAZ

YAYINLARI

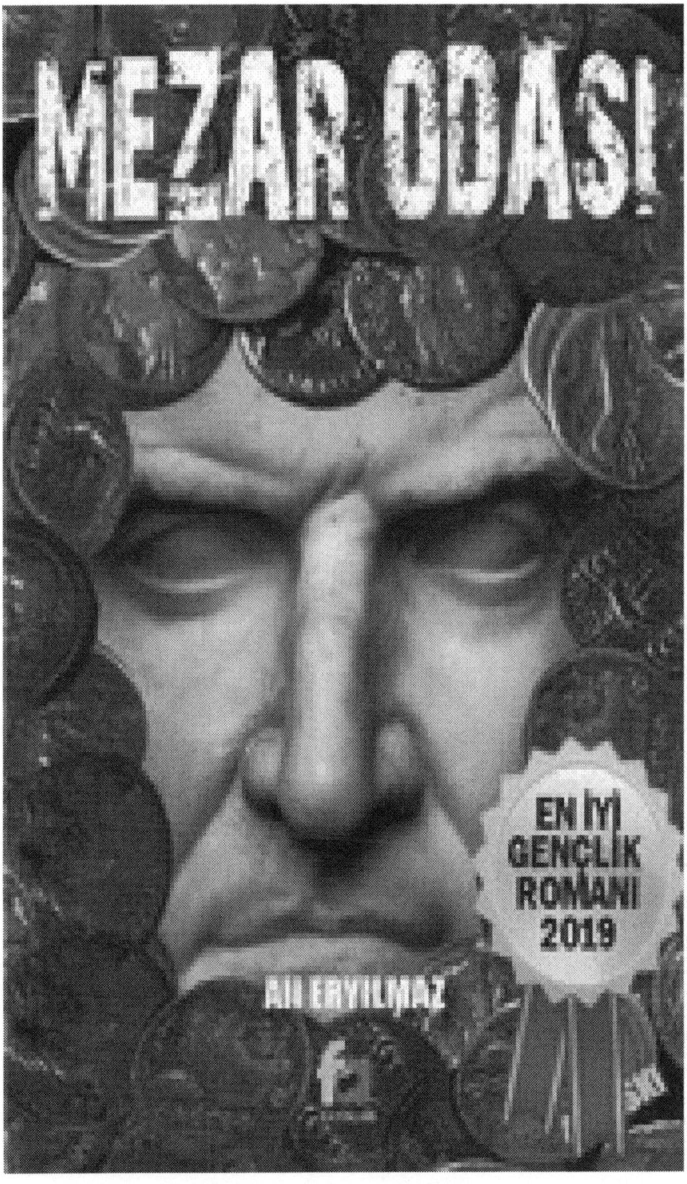
MEZAR ODASI
EN İYİ GENÇLİK ROMANI 2019
ALİ ERYILMAZ

Made in the USA
Las Vegas, NV
13 January 2022

41294654R00113